Reviewer's Co

D0525668

"This is an essential handbook for those involved is an easily accessible resource for leaders, mar and development. As a developer of coaches an myself, and I will be recommending it for the many and varied tools and techniques which can be used to enhance individual as well as organisational performance. There is a good blend of practical exercises which can be used in a range of situations. These are enriched with real case-studies from Mike Wash's extensive experience of leading business excellence in organisations across different cultures. It is clearly written and will be useful at every level in an organisation."

Dr Mary Connor, consultant in individual and organization development

"I like the simplicity and presentation of the material. Mike has managed to provide a succinct summary of each technique that is instantly useable to a 'newcomer' or that rekindles the memory spark for experienced practitioners."

Malcolm Hurrell, Vice President, Human Resources, AstraZeneca

"I like this book very much. It's practical, useful and written in a way that will help support managers to try something new. I think all managers and leaders would benefit from this book. It can be dipped into when required so that when you are confronted with an issue and in need of some creative spirit – you can find out not just 'what' but 'how' to go about dealing with it."

Christopher Philip Bunker, HR Director UK and Ireland, ABS Wastewater Technology Limited

"A good toolkit to get the job done better . . . . taking a spanner instead of a hammer causes fewer damaged pipes; there are some excellent tools in Mike's bag and I particularly like the very simple ones that force me to use diagrams or make choices, so sharpen how I think about an issue."

David Baines, Regional Chairman, Vistage International (UK) Limited

"As someone who is regularly involved with managing and communicating change in large complex organisations, I have found Mike's tools and techniques to be invaluable. I use them everyday in my working and personal life and find they help me to achieve the things I want to achieve."

Suzanne Hughes, Regional Corporate Affairs Manager, Environment Agency – North West

"A good toolkit for managers and professional staff."

Jane Horan, Director, Organisational Development, The Walt Disney Company AP Ltd

"The book has an easy style which will encourage people to read, digest and use. It will have a particular appeal to the public sector."

Professor Tom McGuffog MBE

"It's a great idea to collect so many tools and techniques under one, easy to read book. I wish I had access to this book when I was starting out as a manager. Experienced managers will also find it useful as an aide-memoir."

Lawrence Jackson, Managing Director, Gentech International Limited

"Very readable and a good jogger on what we should know as managers, but readily forget. The case studies help by showing the application and bringing the different points together. Clear, useful and practical!"

Christopher Gibbs, Engineering Director, Cathay Pacific Airways

For a complete list of Management Books 2000 titles
visit our web-site on http://www.mb2000.com

54 TOOLS AND TECHNIQUES FOR BUSINESS EXCELLENCE

Michael Wash

From the simplest 'generation of ideas' to the transformation of organisational culture, these tools and techniques are the essential basics – the 'must do' and the 'must know' of management and business excellence.

2000

First published in 2007 by Management Books 2000 Ltd
Forge House, Limes Road
Kemble, Cirencester
Gloucestershire, GL7 6AD, UK
Tel: 0044 (0) 1285 771441
Fax: 0044 (0) 1285 771055
Email: info@mb2000.com
Web: www.mb2000.com

British Library Cataloguing in Publication Data is available

ISBN 9781852525514

To the Royal Liverpool Children's NHS Trust – Alder Hey and Cathay Pacific Airways. Two organisations who have successfully applied many of the techniques included here and pride themselves in being the best at what they do.

Acknowledgements

None of the approaches outlined in this book are original works. Over the last twenty years I have used, and adapted, these tools and techniques from many esteemed scholars, authors and gurus – too many to mention here.

I am indebted to the contributions they have made and I thank them for allowing practitioners, like myself, to test out their effectiveness.

However, there is one person whose work has influenced me significantly more than others. Thank you to Professor Gerard Egan whom I have, over the years, had the privilege to work with and put his Skilled Helper Model into practice, along with his model for Organisational Change and his helpful description of Shadowside Management.

These have been the basis of my consultancy practice and many of my clients today are usefully putting into practice approaches to improvement based on my interpretation of Professor Egan's models.

George Buchanan, a client and past Chief Executive of several Scottish Health Service Trusts who has encouraged and trusted me to support him in putting many of the Tools and Techniques into practice.

Tony Bell OBE, Chief Executive of Royal Liverpool Children's Hospital, whose constructive feedback and working relationship I have valued greatly over the years. His pioneering application of these approaches have resulted in real benefits in the health of patients.

Rebecca Burke-Sharples CBE, Chief Executive of Halton and St Helen's Primary Care Trust, for her leadership in shaping these approaches to achieve sustainable culture change.

Graham Higgins, whose confidence in me has helped me enrich my career and work experience.

Graham Dexter, who has taught me a lot about true friendship and partnership.

A special mention to Caren Grieves, my PA and Office Manager, who was instrumental in initiating and supporting me in pulling together much of the content and design for this book.

Contents

Contents

Introduction

This book will provide you with easy to follow, practical advice which will enable you to improve your efficiency and effectiveness at work – i.e. improve quality and work smarter!

Every technique described here has been used either in my role as a teacher, facilitator, manager or consultant. I offer them to the reader in a simple, helpful format – because I know they work.

For each of the 54 techniques, you will find the following table:

T&T No:			
Title:			
For use by:			
When to use:			
Also see T&T No:			
Difficulty Rating:		Category:	

This table will provide you with instant information, letting you immediately see your options and focus for the technique you are about to apply.

T&T No: This is the number of the technique. Useful to use when cross referencing with other techniques.

Title: Immediate confirmation of the title of each technique.

For use by: This is to guide the reader as to who may benefit from using this technique.

When to use: Whether in meetings, in team workshops, or in difficult circumstances, this guides you to the best time to apply the particular technique.

Also see T&T no.: This will cross-reference other tools and techniques which can enhance or complement the use and performance of the particular technique.

Difficulty rating: This illustrates a difficulty rating. 1=straight forward, 2=quite easy, 3=moderately hard, 4=challenging, 5=very challenging. However, this rating is only given as a guide and, of course, the principles and guidance given will help reduce the degree of difficulty with practice.

Category: This gives an indication of the area of development that the particular technique relates to.

Once the technique is outlined, there is also provision of an example or illustration to show the best practice of the technique.

Symbols:

💥   This symbol indicates **critical points** throughout each tool or technique.

👫   This symbol indicates **group work** requirement.

✗   This symbol indicates a **priority action point**.

☐   This symbol indicates **note-taking or flipchart required**.

◀»   This symbol indicates a **potential risk or pitfall area**.

DL   This indicates that you have the facility to **download** certain questionnaires and exercises, available from www.54.mwauk.com.

Is This Book For You?

You may be a manager wondering if there is a better or smarter way of managing your team or progressing your projects.

You may be an MBA Student about to graduate and wondering how all this theory works in practice?

It could be that you have just been promoted into a supervisory position and are wondering – what next?

It might be that you have been a manager for some years now and wondering if you are getting a little complacent. Perhaps it's worth brushing up on a few techniques – who knows, there may be something new for you here.

If you are a manager or a professional who has a responsibility in the organisation to facilitate or encourage change – then this is your toolkit!

There are even significant approaches for the executive in senior positions who may have questions about either – can I change the culture of my organisation, or are my managers equipped with the right skills and approaching their job in the most efficient way?

Or, you may be someone in an organisation who just thinks 'there must be a better way to do this!'

How to Use This Book

In any management situation, whether it's a problem to be solved, project to be managed, team to motivate or an individual to coach, it's important – first of all – to assess what is actually going on – i.e. get the facts. (Some of these tools and techniques can help you do this – see section 'What's really going on?').

Management or more precisely – leadership – requires the manager to 'move the situation on' – i.e. manage either by enabling improvement or solving the problem. This requires giving an element of direction or helping others find their own direction. (Tool and Technique numbers 18 and 30 are examples of approaches that help clarify what it is you are trying to achieve).

Following clarity about the situation and the outcome you're looking to achieve, it is important that action plans are formulated (see T&T No 14 and 16). Within the above process (described in more detail in T&T No 20 – Problem Management/Solving) there are many approaches to help the individual or organisation become more excellent at what they do.

This book offers you assistance, not in providing you with solutions, but providing you with methods to find the best way forward for you, your team and your organisation.

So, if you have a focus, area of interest or question – for example, how can I manage my meetings more effectively, how can I be more efficient, how can I improve my presentation skills, how can I delegate more effectively or how can I change my organisation? – then exploring the relevant techniques related to these questions, and more importantly putting them into practice will assist you in your personal quest to become a more effective manager and leader.

'DL' (Download) is indicated on some of the exercises and techniques. This gives you the facility of downloading a specific questionnaire or exercise as part of the technique described, for your own use or to use with your team.

T&T No:	1		
Title:	CAUSE AND EFFECT ANALYSIS		
For use by:	Anyone involved in problem-solving or improvement projects.		
When to use:	Getting to the root cause of problems.		
Also see T&T No:	8, 13, 24, 40		
Difficulty Rating:	2	Category:	(A) Find out 'What's really going on?'

Cause and Effect Analysis

What is it?

Cause and effect analysis is a technique which may be used in improvement projects to identify how different possible causes affect a given problem. Sometimes referred to as the 'Ishikawa' or the 'Fish Bone' diagram.

Why use it?

- To help generate ideas and record them.
- To reveal hidden relationships and highlight important relationships.
- To investigate root causes.

When might it be used in projects?

- Cause and effect analysis is an invaluable aid to project management.
- It is a useful aid to problem management in general.
- It is a useful means to getting a quality improvement group working together in its early history.

Benefits of using cause and effect analysis

- As well as identifying individual causes to problems, groups of causes can be located that are not immediately obvious.

- Use of the technique in a group enables everyone to contribute. In this way, the widest range of expertise can be drawn on.

Developing the cause and effect diagram

1. Establish the effect/problem to be investigated.
2. ☐ On the flipchart or paper draw a box with the effect/problem statement in it.
3. Draw a line extending from the left of the box and identify the main categories of causes (e.g. Manpower, Machinery, Methods, Materials, or develop categories that suit your business).
4. Draw lines extending from the one attached to the box, one for each category.
5. Brainstorm (see T&T No 40) for sub-causes in each category and attach them to the appropriate line. (This can be done using post-its. Move them as the group considers where the causes should lie.)
7. Once the causes are located, lines expressing relationships between the causes can be added, usually in a different colour.

♦ Ground rules for success

- Use large diagrams.
- Ensure everyone's participation.
- Examine relationships between causes.
- Do not overload the diagram:
  - isolate dominant causes.
  - be sure you have defined the problem.
- Do not look for someone to blame.
- Follow brainstorming rules.

Example 1

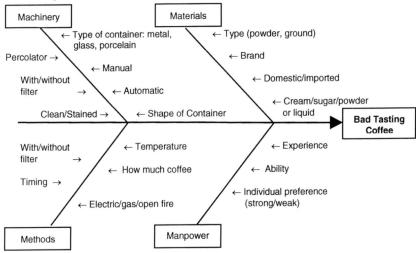

Example 2

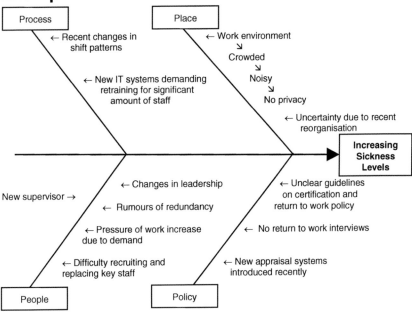

Next step options

It is then possible to 'Pareto' each section (see T&T No 13) and analyse further the item causing most of the effect.

'Why, why, why?' (see T&T No 8) can be a useful way of finding out what's really going on at this stage.

Case study: Cause and Effect

An electrical goods distributor was having a significant increase in goods returned due to inaccurate orders being filled and delivered. This was the responsibility of the order requisition team and the warehouse picking teams.

Representatives from all departments, including sales and order processing, and the warehouse staff were brought together and were helped to construct a cause and effect diagram.

The effect of increased numbers of returns was caused by many different factors, including:-

Materials	– equipment boxes not clearly labelled.
	– shelves too low or too high.
	– box stacking unstable, some spillage, etc.
Manpower	– shift system resented, resulting in poor motivation.
	– lack of measures of productivity.
	– lack of cooperation between departments.
	– poor supervision.
Machinery	– warehouse belt breakdown.
Money	– poor incentive scheme.

This exercise resulted in a number of shop floor changes which were owned and followed through by the staff themselves, resulting in an 80% reduction in order errors.

T&T No:	2		
Title:	CONFLICT MANAGEMENT		
For use by:	Team Leader, Manager		
When to use:	When communication or relationship breakdown is evident or at risk		
Also see T&T No:	12, 34		
Difficulty Rating:	5	Category:	(A) Find out 'What's really going on?'

Conflict Management

CUDSA is a systematic approach to dealing with conflict situations. It is easy to remember, and gives you support in what may be a heated, emotional situation. It is aimed at achieving a 'win-win', positive outcome to conflict. It offers an alternative to escalating resentments and feuds, and enables a rational approach to difficult situations to develop.

If CUDSA is to have maximum effect, you will need to remember to be assertive, non-defensive and non-aggressive in your communication. It is best to leave the physical area where the initial conflict has taken place, to sit down in a neutral area, taking the process as slowly as necessary to gain a 'win-win' outcome. If you are intervening to apply CUDSA in a dispute between two others, calmly assert your authority, and confront any tendency for the dispute to escalate.

CUDSA = Confront the conflict.
Understand each other's position.
Define the problems.
Search for and evaluate alternatives.
Agree on and implement best solution(s).

Step 1 Confront the conflict.
- 💣 Stop the conflict.
- Indicate your desire to resolve the conflict.
- 📢 Identify defensive routines[*].

---

[*] These are behaviours we engage in to protect our position, to rationalise or make excuses for how things are

- Enlist the cooperation of the other party (or parties) to stop the conflict.
- Move to a quiet, private area, if at all possible.
- If this is not an immediate possibility, identify a time and place to meet and sort things out.

Step 2   Understand each other's position.
- Use responding and questioning skills.
- Check understanding regularly.
- Be tentative.
- ⋔ Make no judgements, and do not allow others to berate each other – defuse anger.
- Make sure all parties understand the respective points. Ask them to summarise if necessary.
- Set a reasonable time limit on the discussion.
- Keep reminding yourself you want a positive outcome for all.
- If one person is tending to over-react, postpone things, and talk to them individually.

Step 3   Define the problems.
- Summarise the points from both sides.
- Allow each person to modify the summaries as required.
- Make regular checks for agreement on the summaries.
- Control unfair or intimidating behaviour or remarks.

Step 4   Search for and evaluate alternatives.
- Be explicit that both needs can not be met.
- Encourage/reinforce any attempts to solve the problem.
- Make suggestions, not recommendations, when possible.
- Allow suggestions to be modified.
- Encourage trade-off/negotiation. (See T&T No 12.)
- Make sure the final outcome is acceptable to both parties.

Step 5   Agree on and implement best solution(s).

- View agreement as a contract to be upheld. (See T&T No 34.)
- 🛉 Consider what needs to happen for the solution to be implemented.
- Discuss the mutual benefits of new solution.
- Reinforce/praise the parties involved.
- Offer realistic support to the parties if possible.
- Detail the appropriate plans needed to put new solution into practice.

💣   Working through a 'conflict situation' invariably throws up many powerful emotions. In reality, these processes are many and complex. It may require offering individual support to help diffuse and understand the emotions before moving on. Skilful facilitation and effective interpersonal skills on all sides at each stage are important, if a long lasting agreement and/or a way forward is to be achieved.

Case study: Conflict Management

High sickness rate, patient complaints, delays in admission and discharge and a formal complaint about bullying – these were the presenting symptoms from one particular department in a large hospital. The department was a day patient ward, where quick and caring throughput of morning and afternoon list patients were crucial. This was a very unhappy working environment.

I interviewed most of the staff. The main problems were down to two shift leaders (charge nurses) fighting over control of staff rota and one accusing the other of being unfair. This was complicated by a number of staff recently returning from maternity leave insisting on certain days off – which resulted in a perception of unfairness from the other staff.

The first stage in solving this was to get the two managers responsible to accept that there was a problem and that they were part of it. Bringing them together and exploring differences and the impact they were having on the working environment was a difficult but worthwhile conversation.

This resulted in a commitment to have a ½ day time out with all the staff where a renewed vision of how best to work together took place.

21

Compromise and a reiteration of values were key elements. Significant improvement was evident through a noticeable difference in the ward atmosphere – i.e. more smiles, more cooperation, and more initiative to improve and to be flexible.

T&T No:	3		
Title:	DATA GATHERING AND PRESENTING DATA		
For use by:	Project Manager and Project Team members		
When to use:	When facts are important in establishing what's going on		
Also see T&T No:	19, 20, 22		
Difficulty Rating:	3	Category:	(A) Find out 'What's really going on?'

Data Gathering and Presenting Data

What is it?

Data gathering is an important part of the problem-solving and project management process, both in terms of helping to define the extent of the problem initially, and also in determining whether or not the solution which was implemented has actually achieved what was desired. Data presentation is then the delivery of that data in a format which is readily understood, meaningful and accurate.

When to use it

- At the start of a Quality Improvement Project to help determine the size and extent of a problem.
- When testing a range of solutions to determine the best one to select for implementation.
- After implementation, when monitoring to ensure that the problem has been resolved.
- When reporting to a controlling body on the progress of projects.

What does it achieve?

- Helps to objectively identify the size and scope of the problem (what, when, where, who, etc.).
- Compares the success of a range of solutions to determine the optimum one for implementation.
- Used after implementation, it determines whether or not the problem has actually been solved.
- Helps present data in a format which is readily assimilated by others, enabling objective discussion and choice.

Key steps

- Determine data to be collected.
- Determine optimum method for data collection:
  - Run charts.
  - Sampling.
  - Tally sheets, etc.
- ✓ Determine period over which data is to be gathered.
- Gather data.
- Analyse and evaluate.
- Determine preferred method of data display.
- Create display.

Examples of data display:

Column Bar chart

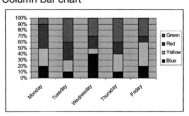

Pie Chart

Scatter Diagram

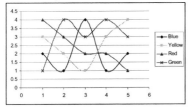

Line Chart

Line Bar Chart

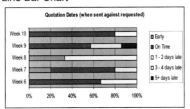

Area Chart

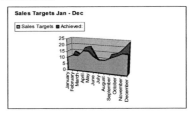

Data gathering guidelines

1. ♦*⏴» Keep it simple. The purpose of analysis is to gain insight, and the best analysis is the simplest analysis which gives clarity.

2. The data gathering exercise should interfere with normal work as little as possible – or not at all.

3. The people who work in the area under investigation should carry out the data gathering (they should be carrying out the investigation anyway).

4. Use Plan–Do–Study–Act on the data-gathering exercise. Determine the scope and purpose before deciding what data to gather. Pilot your data gathering method on a small scale and modify it if necessary.

5. ♦* Gather data before AND after the changes.

6. ⏴» The data gathered should be a reasonable representation of the whole process. It would not be a good idea to gather data over a bank holiday or only on Monday's night shift!

7. Don't reinvent the wheel. If the data you require already exists in a useable format – all you need to do is pick it up. If it doesn't – you will need to design a method of gathering the data.

'If you can't measure it, you can't improve it'

T&T No:	4		
Title:	LADDER OF INFERENCE		
For use by:	Facilitators, Managers challenging assumptions		
When to use:	When getting to the facts is important		
Also see T&T No:	1, 8, 20, 44		
Difficulty Rating:	1	Category:	(A) Find out 'What's really going on?'

The Ladder of Inference

Have you ever been accused of jumping to the wrong conclusion? Or been told to 'get your facts right'?

In an ever faster-paced, pressured world, we can sometimes rush, take short cuts – and in doing so, make assumptions quickly in order to move decisions on or achieve tasks with tight deadlines.

Management by fact, rather than by assumption, requires the discipline of asking for objective data – before embarking upon a course of action that may, if wrong, be very costly.

The ladder of inference – or 2+2 = 5! (Argyris, C., 1990)

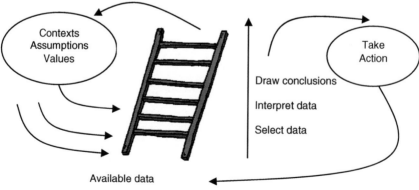

We are so skilled at thinking that we jump up the ladder without knowing it:-

- We tacitly register some data and ignore other data.
- We impose our own interpretations on these data and draw conclusions from them.
- We lose sight of how we do this because we do not think about our thinking.
- Hence, our conclusions feel so obvious to us that we see no need to retrace the steps we took from the data we selected to the conclusions we reached.

The context we are in, our assumptions and our values channel how we jump up the ladder:-

- Our model of how the world works and our repertoire of actions influence the data we select, the interpretations we make and the conclusions we draw.
- Our conclusions lead us to act in ways that produce results that feed back to reinforce (usually) our context and assumptions.

Our skill at reasoning is both essential and gets us into trouble:-

- If we thought about each inference we made, life would pass us by.
- But people can and do reach different conclusions. When they view their conclusions as obvious, no one sees a need to say how they reached them.
- When people disagree, they often hurl conclusions at each other from the tops of their respective ladders.
- This makes it hard to resolve differences and to learn from one another.

So much decision-making, action and conflict is based on assumption rather than fact. Challenging assumptions is an essential requisite to creating a fact based organisation rather than a rumour based one. The following is a version of the Ladder of Inference in practice, start reading from the bottom up, and notice the different interpretations between assumption and fact:-

		Assumption	**Fact**
Level 4	A personal and often biased or prejudicial judgement or assumption based on Level 3.	Senior Management are hypocrites – one rule for them, another for us. They value management posts rather than customers.	Staff officer recruited to reduce bureaucracy and paper system in order to increase speed of complaints procedure.
Level 3	A personal assumption and rationale for Level 2.	Total freeze is not appropriate as there are some appointments that would save us money.	CE Office in the middle of recruiting a staff officer at time of freeze. Completes the appointment.
Level 2	Reasonable and generally acceptable judgement based on Level 1.	Money is tight and recruitment cost high, so this should help.	Overspend by 15%. Recruitment costs amount to 1%.
Level 1	Observable facts based on tangible direct experience.	Recruitment freeze as part of response to severe overspend of budget.	Policy agreed to continue recruitment of posts advertised internally.

Escalating up the ladder of inference is a common process and sometimes the speed of escalation feels like individuals jumping from Level 1 to Level 4. We can see in the example above that someone working on the assumption column will have a different attitude at work than someone working on the facts. Organisations with a rich 'grapevine' or rumour machine are often communicating at level 3 and 4.

♠ The challenge here is to manage by fact. What is the tangible data, the actual event, the facts of the situation? This will require professional, objective, businesslike listening and understanding – qualities that are so often forgotten in the emotive agenda of people championing their particular cause.

T&T No:	5		
Title:	QUESTIONNAIRES		
For use by:	Supervisors, Managers, Facilitators		
When to use:	To establish feedback from staff and/or customers		
Also see T&T No:	3, 25		
Difficulty Rating:	4	Category:	(A) Find out 'What's really going on?'

Questionnaires

Why?

Questionnaires can be a useful way of gathering information from staff (e.g. 'What is it like working here?'), or from customers (e.g. 'Are we meeting your requirements?').

How?

1. ☛ Be clear abut what you want to find out, from whom and why. It is useful to ask yourself, when you get the information, what are you hoping to learn and what do you intend to do as a consequence of the information?

2. Focus on the specifics you want to ask.

3. Decide on the style of questionnaire:
    - Make it simple and easy to complete.
    - ☜ Don't have too many questions. More than 30 questions may be too daunting to a potential responder.
    - Make sure it looks professional.
    - Be clear on the questionnaire – state what it is for, why it is important, and how the data will be used.
    - Reassure confidentiality and/or anonymity, if appropriate.
    - Detail where to return the questionnaire to once it is complete.
    - State an appreciation for the completion of questionnaire/time taken.

- You may want to add an incentive for completion – for example, place the persons name in a draw for a prize – this will require contact information detailing on the form.

4. Decide on the balance between open and closed questions:

Open Questions:
- This gives the responder an opportunity to give relevant feedback in their own words.
- By analysing open statements, themes can be identified.

Closed Questions:
- This is the most popular type of questionnaire format as it gives the responder a forced choice.
- It is simple and efficient – quick to complete.
- Easy to analyse and extract data.
- Easy to report on results.

5. Apply the principle of effective questions:
- Use short and simple sentences.
- Ask for only one type of information at a time.
- Don't ask negative questions.
- Check that the words you are using can not be open to misinterpretation.

6. Types of questionnaire – see examples below.

The 'forced choice' style questionnaire is probably the most popular. 'Ranking' is probably the least as it is more difficult to complete. The 'Likert' style questionnaire is probably favoured due to its ease of use and the option of coding and transferring the data to software for analysis.

Examples

Forced choice (closed) format
Choice of Categories: ❑ Single ❑ Married ❑ Divorced ❑ Widowed

'Likert' Style scale (Likert, R., 1903 – 1981)
'Statistics is an interesting subject'
❑Strongly agree ❑Agree ❑Cannot decide ❑Disagree ❑Strongly disagree

Differential Scales
'How would you rate the presentation?'
  Extremely Interesting 1 2 3 4 5 6 7 8 9 10 Extremely Dull

It may also be diagrammatic – i.e. place a cross on the following to indicate your view:

Extremely Interesting ◄───────────────────────► Extremely Dull

Checklists
'Circle the clinical specialties you are particularly interested in'

General medicine	Obstetrics and gynaecology
General surgery	Orthopaedics
Ophthalmology	Accident and emergency
Paediatrics	General practice

Ranking
'Please rank your interest in the following specialities'
(1 = most interested, 8 = least interested)

General medicine	Obstetrics and gynaecology
General surgery	Orthopaedics
Ophthalmology	Accident and emergency
Paediatrics	General practice

Finally

✆ It is useful to pilot and evaluate a questionnaire before using it on a wider audience. This gives an opportunity to clarify language, avoid ambiguity and test whether the information gathered is what was expected.

T&T No:	6		
Title:	STAKEHOLDER ANALYSIS		
For use by:	All those involved in or influenced by change		
When to use:	Need to influence and increase likelihood of ownership of change		
Also see T&T No:	42		
Difficulty Rating:	3	Category:	(A) Find out 'What's really going on?'

Stakeholder Analysis

Stakeholder analysis is a useful tool to map out the influencing factors related to a particular 'change' or 'project' you are involved in. The reality will be that most issues involve a complex network of relationships between many individuals, most of whom will have an opinion on what you are doing. Managing this matrix of opinion can make the difference between success or otherwise.

Step 1.   Identify a change you wish to make to
- a project you are leading
- a problem you are solving
- a proposal you are making
- a task you have
…one that will need others to implement effectively

Step 2.   List those stakeholders directly involved.

Also identify those who may not be directly involved but potentially important or influential.

Step 3.   Draw your diagram.

Indicate how each of your stakeholders relate to the project and to each other, using the following marks/symbols:

═══════	strong
▬▬▬▬▬	clear
─ ·· ─ · ─ ·· ··	weak

Indicate whether they are:

- supportive of what you want   ☺
- not supportive   ☹
- unsure   ?

Identify:

- the relationships with potential conflict   ♯
- where the powerful people are – usually those   ☺
  with resources or those in positions of significant
  influence

Add your own symbols to describe other issues.

Step 4.   In light of your analysis

What plans do you wish to make to communicate to and influence the stakeholder to increase the likelihood of a successful project or change? (What do you want to communicate, to whom and when?)

It can be useful to categorise your stakeholders in terms of power and interest – by using the following grid:-

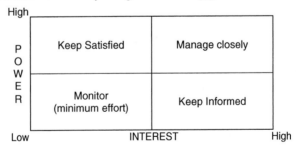

Depending on the complexity of the issue, it may be that you will need several communication plans, with each stakeholder requiring a different approach – for example, politicians will need a well thought through approach with insight into their agenda, while key figures in the community will need to be approached with a sensitivity and awareness of the community agenda.

Following through on a communication plan takes significant time – do not underestimate and ensure you plan for this when allocating resources.

Also, do not take for granted how you are perceived by others. A 360° perception audit can be quite illuminating.

Example of a stakeholder map

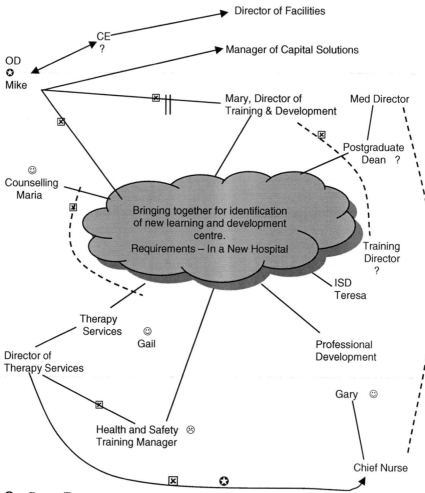

☺ = Power/Resources
☒ = Conflict
☺ = Ally
☹ = Foe
|| = Barriers to communication
? = Fence sitter (could go either way)

T&T No:	7		
Title:	SWOT AND PESTLE ANALYSIS		
For use by:	Managers		
When to use:	To establish internal and external business influences and drivers		
Also see T&T No:	6, 40		
Difficulty Rating:	1	Category:	(A) Find out 'What's really going on?'

SWOT and PESTLE Analysis

SWOT analysis

Simply Brainstorm (see T&T No 40) in each section:-

STRENGTHS	WEAKNESSES
What are you good at? What's your reputation? What do you do well? What's your unique selling point? What advantages do you have? What do customers/colleagues appreciate and value about you?	Where do you need to improve? What do customers complain about?
OPPORTUNITIES	THREATS
Given the 'market' situation and your strengths, what options are there for growth? What are the trends and changes you can take advantage of? What other opportunities are there to enhance your 'business' situation?	What are your competitors doing? What do your shareholders or stakeholders (see T&T No 6) expect/demand? What obstacles do you face?

PESTLE analysis

The SWOT analysis can be enhanced by first completing a PESTLE analysis. This helps identify the drivers or influences affecting the organisation, focusing on the following six types of driver:

Political
Economical
Social
Technology
Legal
Environmental

Political

This includes government policy (national and local) and the influence of major stakeholders. Understanding current and future agendas and how stakeholders interact with each other may have significant impact on your business.

Economical

From the global economy to local markets, the impact of recession and increases in prices will have a direct impact on the pressure to be efficient, to consolidate or invest.

Social

The demographics, trends and population changes/migration can influence marketing strategy, at the least – and overall company direction, at the most.

Technology

Predicting how the fastest and most significant IT or technological developments will impact business is important. Optimum utilisation of up-to-date technology is important. It may be better to get the best out of a recently installed system, rather than forever changing to the latest.

Legal

Considerations about human rights, working directives, safety legislation, tax laws and governance requirements are just a few of the many legal considerations affecting business today.

Environmental

Global warming to a devastating level is inevitable unless companies and individuals take personal responsibility to reduce carbon emissions. Issues relevant to waste and pollution are important factors here.

T&T No:	8		
Title:	WHY? WHY? WHY?		
For use by:	Facilitators, Team Leaders		
When to use:	To drill down to root causes		
Also see T&T No:	1, 20		
Difficulty Rating:	1	Category:	(A) Find out 'What's really going on?'

Why? Why? Why?

What is it?

The Why, why, why? technique is a systematic and probing form of questioning designed to get to the root causes and effects in a problem-solving situation.

When to use it

It is most useful when a group or team are working on the detailed analysis of a problem and investigating its causes and effects. The technique can generate a large amount of information.

Time required

Approximately 1 hour.

☐ ♔ Resources required

1.   Flipchart.
2.   Marker pens.

Key steps

1. Create a relaxed and participative atmosphere.
2. Identify the problem to be investigated.
3. Repeatedly ask a series of 'why?' questions to get to root causes/effects (see detailed instructions below).
4. Display results of questions diagrammatically.
5. Reflect on and discuss data generated.

⚑ Detailed instructions when working in a group

1. Because repeated questioning can become tedious for group members, it is important to have created a lively and relaxed atmosphere through the use of ice-breakers and warm-ups. Set groundrules and explain the technique.
2. Identify the problem to be investigated and write it on the left hand side of the board/flipchart.
3. Ask group members why the problem occurs and record all the answers given in the format shown on the diagram.
4. Repeat the process as many times as is necessary to get to the point when the group can no longer give answers.
5. Display the results so that all members can see them and encourage them to reflect on the information.
6. Discuss the explanations generated and try to assess their relative importance in terms of future action. (Pareto analysis may be useful here – see T&T 26.)
7. Review the effectiveness of the technique with the group.

Example

PROBLEM	1ST LEVEL	2ND LEVEL	3RD LEVEL	4TH LEVEL
		Because public transport is insufficient. WHY?	Because of increased privatisation. WHY?	ETC
	Because they have no convenient transport. WHY?	Because they have insufficient money to pay for taxis. WHY?	Because pensions don't keep up with inflation. WHY?	ETC
Elderly people don't take advantage of health clinics. WHY?				
	Because they are not aware of what health clinics are about. WHY?	Because low expectations. WHY?	Because of tradition and experience. WHY?	ETC
		Because health education (HE) doesn't reach them. WHY?	Because HE often not targeted for the elderly. WHY?	ETC
PROBLEM	1ST LEVEL	2ND LEVEL	3RD LEVEL	4TH LEVEL

✦ The major difficulty which can arise with this technique is that the repeated questions can become irritating; facilitators need to be flexible and sensitive in the way they use their questioning skills. It is also important for facilitators to keep the group to the task in hand and avoid getting drawn into discussion of the responses until the exercise is complete.

✦ Following this exercise, the facilitator must refocus the group's attention on **the deepest root cause that they have influence over**. For instance, in the above example, the group can not remove poverty of the elderly, but it can assist with providing the cheapest form of transport.

The technique can be quite challenging when applied to one individual's problem and therefore needs to be used flexibly and supportively – i.e. good listening and understanding as well as the direct 'why' probes.

T&T No:	9		
Title:	DEPARTMENT PURPOSE ANALYSIS		
For use by:	Department Managers, Executives, Chief Executives		
When to use:	To clarify department direction and priorities		
Also see T&T No:	11, 13, 20, 21, 22, 23, 26, 27, 52		
Difficulty Rating:	5	Category:	(B) Be focused, prioritise

Department Purpose Analysis

What is it?

A technique to identify and then clarify the role a department has in supporting the overall mission and vision of the organisation.

It should identify the core purpose, priorities and objectives of the department, then identify the problems or blocks to the department's full effectiveness and use this information to assist the department's quality improvement process.

How to do it

Stage 1   Identification of core purpose, priorities and objectives

a)   ▙▙ The department's top team should decide how it can best contribute to the organisation's strategic goals.   This may be reinforced by putting it in the 'business plan' as a department mission statement. (See T&T No 11.)

b)   The department's top ten activities should be prioritised in line with criteria of the mission statement.

c)   These ten objectives then need to become visible by becoming part of people's personal objectives, reflected in job profiles and in decision-making.

Stage 2   Data gathering

a)   A comprehensive survey of customer and supplier requirements of the department using appropriate measures.

b)   Appraisal (quality control), failure and prevention costs (see T&T No 26) within the department, and from its customer and supplier relationships (see T&T No 27) all need to be clearly identified.

c)   Process analysis (see T&T No 21) of key department activities to uncover hidden costs or improvement opportunities is another important element of understanding current levels of efficiency.

d)   A comprehensive survey of personnel skills and development needs will identify shortfalls and training needs for staff.

Stage 3   Problem identification and Pareto analysis

a)   Department's top team assimilate data in the light of the identified key activities.

b)   Data examined in terms of:
  i.   major failures.
  ii.   direct impact on the quality of working life in the department.
  iii.   opportunities for immediate performance improvement.
  iv.   inappropriate use of resources (e.g. duplication of effort).
  v.   Pareto effect (i.e. which failure activities have the widest effect in terms of compromising or blocking effectiveness in other related activities.) (See T&T No 13.)

c)   ⚡ Project improvement teams and leaders are chosen and improvement goals formulated in project proposals. (See T&T No 23 and 22.)

Stage 4   Quality improvement team actions (long term quality improvement)

a)   Project teams are assigned a facilitator and receive appropriate coaching in project management and other problem-solving tools and techniques. (See T&T No 20.)

b)   Regular improvement team meetings are scheduled. (See T&T No 52.)

c)   Department's top team meet regularly to review, progress and make visible improvement measures and achievements.

Outline of department purpose analysis (summary of stages 1 to 4)

1. Clarify the Vision and purpose of department in the context of Company Vision and strategic priorities.
2. Seek customer feedback from those departments you deliver a service to.
3. Analyse how you spend your time currently in terms of prevention, appraisal and failure. (See T&T 26.)
4. Identify and track the main process flows, for example from goods in to goods out, receiving customer request to despatch, identification of new product to entry into the market place.
   a) Identify each step and highlight opportunities for more efficient flow of information and/or service.
   b) Calculate the potential saving (time and actual).
6. Bring all the above data together and ask to what extent your activities match your priorities.
7. Identify the key areas for improvement and select appropriate teams to apply problem-solving and project management in these areas.
8. Set up an ongoing review and measurement process.

Case study: Department Purpose Analysis (DPA)

A personnel department in a large insurance and investment company was facing a two-pronged challenge. On one hand, due to a merger, it was faced with a significant increase in workload and on the other hand, it was told to reduce in size.

This required a radical rethink. No longer could it continue to fulfil its traditional personnel supplier role. The senior personnel team took time out to reiterate its vision, mission and values. From this, their priorities were set. A key enabling priority was to shift from being personnel managers to HR consultants! This required a shift in understanding across the company, not only what the now called 'HR Department' would be doing, but also, the need for managers to take more responsibility in all matters 'personnel'. The new HR team decided to talk to all departmental managers to inform them of the change, but at the same time, seek feedback as to what sort of support the managers needed.

From the internal customer data, priorities from a customer perspective were matched against HR business plan perspective. This resulted in a well communicated plan of action which not only eased the merger process, but began to re-educate managers and HR staff in a different way of operating.

T&T No:	10		
Title:	KIDS		
For use by:	Teams or individuals evaluating the effectiveness of action		
When to use:	Team view on what's going on		
Also see T&T No:	7, 13, 40		
Difficulty Rating:	1	Category:	(B) Be focused, prioritise

KIDS

This is a simple way of quickly diagnosing or assessing the views of a team about the activities, projects or issues within a department or organisation. An effective and dynamic way of conducting this exercise is in 4 groups.

👥 ☐ Each group to stand by a flipchart in each corner of a room. Give 5 to 10 minutes to brainstorm (see T&T No 40) under the following headings (one for each group/flipchart):

Keep
Improve
Develop
Scrap/Stop

After the allotted time, each group to move round the room to the next flipchart/heading and continue to add to the previous groups list, until each group has contributed to each heading.

Keep

Don't fix it if it's not broken! Whatever is going well, keep doing it. It may be basic or core business, it may be what your reputation is built upon – the danger is in taking it for granted or becoming complacent. It is sometimes useful to highlight the good things and celebrate the success.

Improve

Identify areas of weakness. Areas of work or projects that are important and must not be allowed to fail. This could be 'soft' areas such as relationships, communication or teamwork, or 'hard' areas such as systems, machinery, equipment, tools etc.

Develop

Identify new things needed in order to improve or stay competitive. These could be new markets, skills, networks, relationships, or any tangible resources requiring investment.

Scrap/Stop

These activities are those which are not adding value, are wasting time and/or resources. They may be traditional, historical or just not important as customers and organisations need change.

Case study: KIDS

The following is the result of a KIDS exercise held with a 'water pump' company.

KEEP
• Current momentum
• UK identity
• Service response
• Challenging
• Team Meetings and briefings
• Approachability/customer service
• Achieving targets
• Staff/strong teams
• Customers perception (nice people)
• Customers/frameworks

- Euro hub/UK Hub
- Innovation/positive thinking
- Open culture
- Communicating
- Service centre locations and seek to develop new ones as appropriate
- MDP process
- Appraisal and relevant training
- Accurate financial packs ☺
- Challenging ourselves and each other
- Providing feedback both positive and negative
- Treating each other as customers
- Existing customers
- Searching for new customers
- Customer relationship
- Good staff development
- Staff morale
- Products – Solution providing/packages, market focus, innovation, continuous product improvement

IMPROVE

- The way in which we capture and disseminate customer feedback
- The way in which we work/promote/reward innovation and change
- IT Support systems
- Inter-departmental communications
- Brand image in front of customers
- Inter-departmental systems practices
- Top → Bottom communication
- Bottom → Top communication
- More Group 'Aware'
- Intranet awareness
- Meeting (quality and agenda) to ensure attendance and output (including time management) is maximised
- Environmental performance
- Product awareness
- Contribution
- Quality
- Customer relationships/database
- Administration – best collation?/order process etc
- People development
- Customer facing time
- Time Management/Resource utilisation

DEVELOP

- Energy project – company standard
- Apprentice scheme/Companywide
- Suggestion scheme (innovation and change)
- Cross-fertilization (internally and externally)
- Career development programme
- Best practice skills transfer
- People skills – to support vision/business goals
- Internal systems to support vision/growth
- Succession planning
- New markets/customer feedback
- Customer seminars/training
- People skills/development
- Internal systems to support vision

SCRAP/STOP

- 'Unhealthy' competition between departments (e.g. service and sales)
- Excuses (poor ones) to customers
- No continuous improvement within business, to remedy issue
- Stop avoiding the issue of IT (i.e. take action and communicate this)
- Stop accepting mediocrity (i.e. take responsibility and ownership for problems/issues we see)
- Duplication of resources/processes
- Waiting for others to take the initiative
- Resisting change
- Giving credit to non-credit worthy customers
- Email exhaustion!
- Dual branding products
- Duplication of resources/processes
- Using old brand
- Stop unnecessary archiving
- Wasting paper (e.g. printing emails)
- Quotes – stop wasting time – be more selective
- Products – promoting those we don't sell

From the above lists, the management team were asked to 'Pareto' the top 3. (See T&T No 13.)

KIDS – Rated as Top 3 from each category

KEEP

1. Customer
   - existing
   - searching for new
   - relationship

2. Staff
   - good staff
   - development
   - morale

3. Products
   - solution providing/packages
   - market focus
   - innovation
   - continuous improvement

IMPROVE

1. IT Support systems
2. Top→Bottom/Bottom→Top Communication
3. The way we disseminate customer feedback

DEVELOP

1. People/Skills Development
   - best practice skills transfer
   - apprentice scheme
2. Energy Project
3. Internal Systems to support Vision

STOP

1. 'Unhealthy' competition between departments (e.g. service and sales)
2. Accepting mediocrity – i.e. take responsibility and ownership for problems/ issues we see
3. Duplication of resources/processes

This resulted in identifying a number of improvement projects as well as significant discussion around priorities for future investment and growth.

T&T No:	11		
Title:	MISSION STATEMENTS		
For use by:	Department Heads, Executives		
When to use:	When there is a need to clarify direction or enhance identity/brand		
Also see T&T No:	30		
Difficulty Rating:	2	Category:	(B) Be focused, prioritise

Mission Statements

What is a mission statement?

This is a simple, clear, unambiguous statement about the business you are in. It describes clearly the business purpose and strategic intent.

Why is it important?

It provides identity and focus for everyone working in the organisation. It aids in communicating and educating customers and potential customers what you offer. It can add real value and become part of a brand that people recognise.

What's involved?

The elements of a good mission statement include:-
- Who you are.
- What you do.
- Who for?
- To what standard?

For example: 'MWA is a training and consultancy company that helps individuals and organisations realise their potential to be leaders.'

⬚ A simple, challenging exercise for your team:

Step 1   Describe what a mission statement is and why it is important to have one.

Step 2   Ask each individual in a meeting to write down, without consultation, what they think is the company's mission statement.

Step 3   Circulate them so that everyone reads each others answer. (Collect the written answers each time). For dramatic effect, you could tear up the answers each time and place them in the bin. A mission statement of worth should be engraved in the mind and heart!

Step 4   Repeat this exercise, at least twice, perhaps three times.

Step 5   ⬚ Ask for a volunteer to write the mission statement now, as he/she sees it after reading the teams' versions three times.

Step 6   Discuss the statement – does it fit?

Step 7   Agree for someone to take it away, refine and circulate until there is consensus that the mission statement fits.

✦ This exercise can determine:
- Is there a shared understanding?
- Is there major differences in what the business focus should be?
- What sense of identity do we have?
- How are we seen in the market place?
- Are our staff clear about the business we are in?
- Can we communicate clearly and simply to our customers?

Mission statements are usually easy to remember. Some companies underpin their Mission Statement with a phrase that characterises the essence of what they are about, such as:
- Putting people first.
- Service straight from the heart.
- Caring for and about people.
- We're getting there.

- The people's choice.
- The bank that likes to say yes.
- The listening bank.
- and so on...

Case study: Mission Statements

Cablex were a medium size company supplying all sizes/types of cable to manufacturers, utilities and electrical goods suppliers. They had recently recovered from a damaging dispute with their 'staff side' union, and had lost a large contract with an electrical company to a competitor.

The senior team were unhappy and there seemed to be a need to take stock of the situation.

I was asked to support what was meant to be a half day meeting to ensure everyone was clear about priorities for the coming year, at the same time, create a positive top team atmosphere.

Half way through the morning, I had a suspicion that there was some confusion as to what the main priority of the business should be.

I decided to run the 'mission building' exercise detailed in this technique (T&T No 11). This resulted in the Managing Director and Finance Director having a robust debate as to whether the company direction should be cable manufacturing or cable distribution and servicing.

There was no compromise at the meeting, and although the meeting ended positively, the most significant thing that transpired was that the two key people at the top disagreed as to what should be the core business.

This was, in effect, the source of much unease and poor or delayed decision-making, which resulted in lost business. Eventually, the Finance Director left the company.

T&T No:	12		
Title:	NEGOTIATION SKILLS		
For use by:	Supervisors, Sales, Managers		
When to use:	When you need something from someone else		
Also see T&T No:	34, 35, 44		
Difficulty Rating:	4	Category:	(B) Be focused, prioritise

Negotiation Skills

The best outcome of negotiation is where each party goes away believing they have a 'win' deal – i.e. a 'win-win' situation. This type of agreement is one that is more likely to stick, harbour positive relationships, contributes to a developing partnership and trust.

A win-lose negotiation – i.e. one where one party gains at the expense of the other – may foster resentments, mistrust and an unequal relationship which can be very limiting.

Here, we describe 6 stages of effective negotiation:

STAGES	SKILLS ✊
1. Preparation	Gaining Rapport
2. Arguing	Listening
3. Signalling	Understanding
4. Proposing	Questioning
5. Bargaining	Challenging
6. Closing and Agreeing	Clarifying

Stage 1.   Preparation

Set out your objectives in the negotiation.

Own Interest:
- L – Like-to-get or ideal outcome.
- I – Intend-to-get, or realistic agreement.
- M – Must-get, the point at which you can not compromise.

Identify other's interests:
- L – What are they likely to want, ideally?
- I – What might they settle upon?
- M – What's really important to them?

What are the bridging factors that would make an agreement possible?

What will you have to give, or what have you to give, to promote an agreement?

What fallback positions do you have in case of difficulties?

In what order do you intend to present your propositions?

💣 It is important to be clear about what you want *before* you enter into negotiation. 'Start with the end in mind.'

Good negotiation demonstrates high-level interpersonal skills, including good listening and understanding of the other party's position.

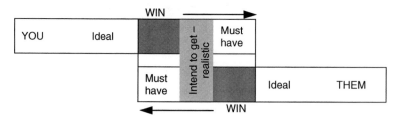

Stage 2. Checklist for arguing

◀▸ Avoid:	Practise:
• Interrupting	• Listening
• Point-scoring	• Questioning for clarification
• Attacking	• Summarising issues neutrally
• Blaming	• Challenging opponent to
• Being 'too clever'	justify his case on an item-by-
• Talking too much	item basis (watch for signals)
• Shouting your opponent down	• Being non-committal about his positions (looking for clues about his priorities)
• Sarcasm	• Seeking and giving
• Threats	information (be careful about unintended signals)

Stage 3. Signalling

The Hidden Language of Signals:

◀▸ What is said:	What this could mean:
'We would find it extremely difficult to meet that deadline.'	*Not impossible.*
'Our production line is not set up to cope with this requirement.'	*But it can be changed.*
'I am not empowered to negotiate this price.'	*See my boss.*
'It is not our normal practice to give discounts.'	*So who's normal.*
'Our company never negotiate on price.'	*We do negotiate what you get for that price.*
'We can discuss that point.'	*It's negotiable.*
'We are not prepared to discuss that at this stage.'	*It's negotiable – tomorrow.*

'We never admit liability.'   *We only make ex gratia payments.*

'We could not produce that quantity in that time.'   *I'm prepared to negotiate on price, delivery, quality, quantity.*

'It is not our policy to give discounts and even if we did they would not be as large as 10 per cent.'   *I'll give you 2 per cent.*

'Our price for that quantity is x.'   *Different quantity, different price.*

'These are our standard contract terms.'   *They're negotiable.*

'That is an extremely reasonable price.'   *It is our most favoured position.*

Stage 4. Checklist for proposing

- Propositions beat arguments because arguments cannot be negotiated.
- What therefore is being proposed, either by yourself or your opponent?
- A proposition is one solution to a conflict: consider the other solutions.
- Do you gain more from linking individual issues in your proposition than from separating them? By linking them you maintain negotiating room later on. By separating them you narrow the negotiating room. This is to your advantage when some items in the conflict are already close to your limit and leaving them linked may force you to make concessions beyond your limit.
- Be firm on generalities like 'We must have compensation.'
- Be flexible on specifics like 'We propose £10,000 compensation'
- Do not use weak language, such as 'hope', 'We like', 'We prefer'. Use strong language like 'We need', 'We must have', 'We require'.
- State your conditions first and be specific.
- Follow with your proposition and be tentative.
- Opening concessions should be small rather than large.
- Opening conditions should be large rather than small.

Stage 5. Checklist for bargaining

- Absolutely firm rule – no exceptions at all, ever: **EVERYTHING MUST BE CONDITIONAL.**
- Decide what you require in exchange for your concessions.
- List and place your requirements at the front of your presentation.
- Signal what is possible if, and only if, they agree to your conditions.
- If the signal is reciprocated present your proposals, re-stating your conditions.
- Keep all the unsettled issues linked and trade-off a move on one for a new condition or a move on something else.
- Be ready to bring back into connection any previously 'settled' issues if you need negotiating room under pressure of opposition on a point.

Stage 6. Checklist for closing and agreeing

- Decide where you intend to stop conceding.
- Is it credible? Is it too soon for your opponent?
- Which close is more appropriate?
- Have they replied 'yes' to a question from you about whether a concession on your part on some item will cause them to agree to the package? (If they say 'no', you must get all of their objections out before making any more concessions.) If they have said 'yes' consider the concession close.
- Think whether to lead with the summary close and then try the concession close or vice versa.
- What other close could you use?
- If you are going for a 'final offer' are you serious or is it a bluff? Remember, a final offer increases in credibility the more formal it is, the more senior the person delivering it, the more public the audience, the more specific it is and the more specific the time for acceptance. Bluffing 'final offers' can destroy credibility in the current negotiations and in subsequent ones. Do not try to force a 'final offer' under emotional pressure.
- Remember: adjournment and or else closes have greater risk in them than concession and summery closes (and either/or closes).
- If the close has been successful: what has been agreed?

- List the agreement detail.
- List the points of explanation, clarification, interpretation and understanding.
- Try to prevent your 'opponent' leaving the table until an agreed summary has been recorded.
- If there is disagreement on an alleged agreement the negotiations must recommence until agreement is reached again.
- If the agreement is oral, send a written note to your 'opponent' of what you believe was agreed as soon as you can after the meeting.

T&T No:	13		
Title:	PARETO ANALYSIS		
For use by:	All		
When to use:	When you need to prioritise		
Also see T&T No:	22, 26		
Difficulty Rating:	1	Category:	(B) Be focused, prioritise

Pareto Analysis

What is it?

Pareto analysis is a tool which is used to prioritise problems in a rank order so that resources can be focused on the 'vital few' causes rather than the 'trivial many' factors which give rise to a problem of problems.

The process based on a general principle proposal by an Italian economist, Vilfredo Pareto (1848–1923). In Juran (1964), it states that 20 percent of the causes have 80 percent of the impact. It has become know as the 80:20 rule. An example of this is that 20% of students make 80% of the contributions in class, or 80% of the wealth in most countries is held by 20% of the population.

The process enables a focus on problems by determining where attention should be directed and the order in which problems should be tackled to gain maximum benefit for effort expended.

When to use it

- To separate the few major problems that cause the effect from the many possible causes, so that improvement efforts can be properly focused.
- To categorise the priority causes and/or data.
- To determine which causes are most important using qualitative data and not intuition or perception.
- Pareto is a tool useful in deciding on a leverage point as part of Stage 2 of a Project Way of Working. (See T&T No 22.)

Key steps

1. Introduce the general principle underlying the process, ie the 80:20 rule.
2. ⚜ Brainstorm the categories, problems or issues to be studied.
3. Decide the criteria to be used when analysing the problem (e.g. cost, frequency of occurrence, impact on staff or customers).
4. Prioritise the criteria on the basis of those giving greater impact.
5. Graphically represent the group findings on the chart.
6. ⟋ Develop an action plan, based on addressing the 20% which will affect the 80%.

Case study: Pareto Analysis

The following list is as a result of brainstorming 'failure activities' (see T&T No 26) in a management team of a national chain of bakers/confectioners. Each individual involved was then asked to identify three items that they think are creating the greatest amount of failure in terms of cost (wasted time, resources, customer dissatisfaction, etc.). The results were collated and a discussion took place to clarify the most significant 'Pareto' items.

Pareto Failure Activities

• High bread waste	5 votes
• Lack of Planning	4 votes
• Large turnover of staff	3 votes
• Too much duplication	3 votes
• New policies – poorly thought out	2 votes
• Poorly trained customer service staff	2 votes
• Lack of open communication	2 votes
• Gaps in the production/communication line	2 votes
• Indecision – revisiting policy	2 votes
• Lack of training	2 votes
• IT equipment – accessibility/compatibility	2 votes

The following two items, because they were seen as significant, were subject to wider debate and resulted in significant improvement initiatives.

- Lack of training.
- Lack of open communication.

Further analysis of the top item – high bread waste – resulted in a national initiative resulting in significant savings.

Pareto Principle applied to Cost of Quality
(see T&T No 26)

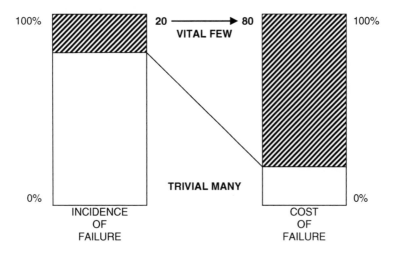

T&T No:	14		
Title:	ACTION PLANS		
For use by:	Project Leader/Supervisor		
When to use:	To advance change		
Also see T&T No:	6, 13, 17, 18, 22, 26, 30		
Difficulty Rating:	3	Category:	(C) Better Project Management

Action Plans

What is it?

An action plan is an outline of who will do what, when and how to achieve a specific objective. Most action plans suffer from inertia (no start) or entropy (fall apart). This is because the first few steps for success have not been thought through in enough detail and personal commitment to act is minimal. Good actions plans will deal with this.

When to use it?

An action plan indicates what needs to be done, by when and by whom; and in particular, it can be used to:

- Co-ordinate the communication of a key message or implementation plan.
- Plan the implementation of a project.
- Plan the implementation of a problem solution.
- Co-ordinate an activity such as data collection.
- Any aspect of change linked to an objective.

Context/Purpose

It is important that actions follow analysis or diagnosis of what is really going on. The vision must be clarified, and then the goal, before actions are designed. **Actions should be goal-directed.** (See T&T No 18 and 30.)

What does it achieve?

Assembling together the action requirements, in terms of: people involvement, resources needed and any special dependencies into an easily understood plan will help you to:

- Decide on priorities.
- Establish any inter-relationships. (See T&T No 6.)
- Assign responsibilities.
- Establish 'required by' dates.
- Review and monitor progress.

☛ By communicating the plan appropriately from the outset, you will help everyone involved to know what is required of them, and by when. This will reduce resistance to change and defensiveness, and increase the likelihood of ownership by the end user.

Key steps

- Involve those responsible for its successful delivery.
- Involve a sample of those who are likely to be affected.
- Ensure understanding of the implication of the change.
- Establish what needs to be done by when.
- Determine dependencies (those resources or actions needed for each stage).
- Communicate information (supported by a communication plan).
- Monitor and review (with clear measures for success).

Template

Sample action plan template

Action Statement	Intended Outcome	Achieved by when (and/or milestones)	Led by	Other significant players and resource dependencies	Customer/Supplier involvement	Related to what overall objective or vision
Set up meeting to get agreement to implement a revised version of the Performance Management System	More consistent, fair and rewarding staff appraisal.	6 months from date/agreement	HR Director	All Personnel Managers and Directors Resource: Budget for training	Internal customers = all staff Suppliers = all managers who conduct appraisals	Better working environment, higher motivated staff. Achievement of Investors in People Award (IIP)

👫 + ⬜ *Prioritising Actions*

When faced with a situation that involves many different actions, it can be useful to organise these actions by using the following matrix:

This analysis may help you inform where best to focus limited resources first. Other criteria to use can be 'which actions are those that are easiest to do that will give the greatest benefit?' (See T&T No 13.)

Case study: Action Plans

Rendex is a 'wiring harness company' which supplies electrical circuits for the motor trade. In reviewing productivity levels at their regular operational review meeting, one member asked why the agenda very rarely changes – i.e. the same problems keep reappearing.

On further enquiry, it transpired that although there was agreement as to actions, they were rarely followed through due to a misunderstanding of who leads and the status of the action in terms of its priority.

The Engineering Director decided to introduce the discipline of action planning, which transformed the way minutes of the meetings were produced. Each action item had a name (who is lead responsible – *only one person*) and a date by when to expect completion.

This resulted in an increase in productivity and a reduction in meeting time.

T&T No:	15		
Title:	COST BENEFIT ANALYSIS		
For use by:	Project Proposers, Change Managers		
When to use:	When putting a case forward for change or evaluating change		
Also see T&T No:	1, 24		
Difficulty Rating:	3	Category:	(C) Better Project Management

Cost Benefit Analysis

What is it?

Cost benefit analysis is a technique for comparing the costs of taking a particular course of action with the benefits achievable from the outcome. It is a method of assessing the viability of the course of action in financial terms.

When to use it

It is important – when selecting a course of action to take – to understand the direct costs and aspired benefits. This can be used as major criteria for success. A cost benefit exercise is often undertaken as part of building a business case for investment in organisations.

What does it achieve?

In solving any problem, it is necessary to consider the effects of the solution. It is of little benefit if the costs of the planned actions far outweigh the benefits achieved.

Cost benefit analysis will help a team decide whether to proceed with a proposed solution on cost grounds, or to seek a better one.

It can also be used to compare, in money terms, a number of problem solutions or plans of action.

Key steps

- Determine the period of analysis.
- Determine the cost factors (initial and ongoing).
- Value the benefits (immediate, medium and long term).
- ✗ Analyse and evaluate the information.

Note:

✒ Costs are either one-off, or may be ongoing. Benefits are most often achieved over time. (See illustration below.) Costs are often direct, like material or capital investment costs – or indirect, like the cost of project managing, re-training, salaries, etc.

Benefits can be either tangible (such as increased speed of transaction, or increased customer satisfaction leading to increased sales) or intangible (such as increased motivation and teamwork).

Benefit over time

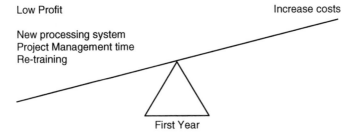

Low Profit

Increase costs

New processing system
Project Management time
Re-training

First Year

Leading to: an increase in accuracy of inventory
an increase in speed of information
less duplication of spares
constant and more accurate up-to-date storage information

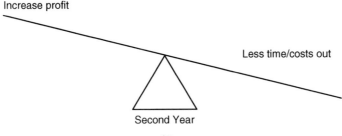

Increase profit

Less time/costs out

Second Year

♦⃰ The greater the expenditure and the longer the payback period, the greater the need to recognise the value of expert help from a reputable financial advisor!

Case study: Cost Benefit Analysis

Within a large telecommunications company, it was decided to invest in a new central stores system to enable more efficient stocking, ordering and issuing of customers installation and repair kits.

This was a multi-million pound investment. The decision was made easier by analysing the cost of the current systems, this included:

- increasing number of customer complaints.
- increasing number of staff complaints.

In addition to this, the engineers' confidence in the current system was low, so they were building their own stock and stores in their own vans, yards and homes. This resulted in a significant amount of outdated and surplus stock.

Engineers were also running a thriving private business using untraceable, surplus and outdated stock to fulfil neighbours home telephone installation, extension and repair requests.

The costs of these activities outweighed the costs of installing a new system.

Costs of implementing the new system included the re-training of staff and the opportunity to realign personal and company values was taken.

T&T No:	16
Title:	CRITICAL PATH ANALYSIS and FLOWCHARTING
For use by:	Project Improvement Members
When to use:	To clarify key tasks within a project
Also see T&T No:	21
Difficulty Rating:	3	Category:	(C) Better Project Management

Critical Path Analysis and Flowcharting

What is it?

Critical path analysis (CPA) is a technique for analysing the work to be done on a project or change process into identifiable tasks over a period of time.

When to use it

CPA can be used on any project (large or small) which has a definable beginning and end and involves the performance of a number of distinct but interrelated tasks, according to a logical sequence of work flow.

What does it achieve?

CPA enables parallel courses of action to be examined throughout the life of the project. As a result, communications are improved, trouble-spots are highlighted for special attention at the right time, and effort is concentrated on the time-critical tasks. Overlap and potential competing points for reference can be seen ahead of the event and planned for. Possible downtime and slippage are identified in advance, which allows other activities in the critical path to be brought forward or rescheduled, thus 'taking up the slack' and enabling the job to be delivered on time.

Key steps

Stage 1
- ☐ List activities.
- Note constraints.
- Draw Network.

Stage 2
- Add time estimates for activities.
- Calculate float, critical path, etc.

Stage 3
- Agree network and target dates.
- Modify network if necessary.
- Distribute networks or issue data.

Stage 4
- ✗ Monitor progress.
- Initiate remedial action if necessary.

Example

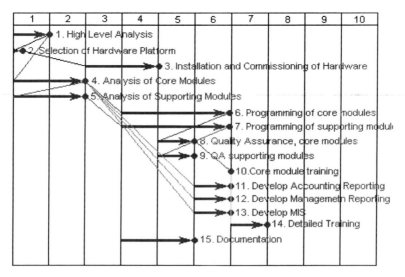

Ref: http://www.psywww.com/mtsite/critpath.html

Flowcharting

This is a tool for recording clearly a series of events or activities in any process. It takes a diagrammatic form, which can be easily understood and communicated. Flowcharts can be used to enhance a critical path diagram.

Accurate flowcharts can be powerful tools in stimulating change (see T&T No 21). If any improvements are to be made, first of all, the existing process needs clearly identifying. Careful analysis will identify opportunities for quality improvement, which also reduce costs and increase efficiency.

Using a few standard symbols can produce an effective diagrammatic representation of the process:

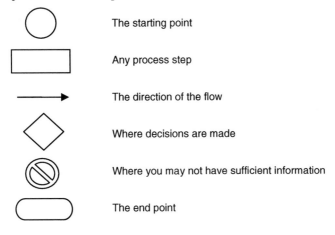

The starting point

Any process step

The direction of the flow

Where decisions are made

Where you may not have sufficient information

The end point

No one individual can produce an accurate flowchart. It is important to involve everyone who is involved in the process to reveal the true process.

Undertaking flowcharting of an activity will not only improve knowledge of the process but will also begin to develop the teamwork, which is necessary in any process improvement endeavour.

When starting a flowchart it is important to agree on the first and last steps, to provide a boundary for the process.

There may be steps, which are uncertain, and then it is necessary to go out and gather information, later.

Issues and Improvement ideas may well be generated during the flowcharting process. It is important to record these for later consideration.

71

The discussion during the process is often as important as designing the flowchart itself.

By using 'post-it' notes on a flowchart, stages can easily be modified in the light of new information.

💣 It is important to examine each symbol and ask if it is necessary. You will probably identify several re-work loops in a flowchart – is it necessary? Does it prevent problems from occurring? What is the cost? Delays need also to be examined with regard to their length.

Once the original process has been identified on a flowchart, succeeding flowcharts should be drawn to show how the process could be improved. Therefore in terms of a quality improvement process, flowcharts can be used at every stage.

Example of a flowchart used in problem-solving/decision-making

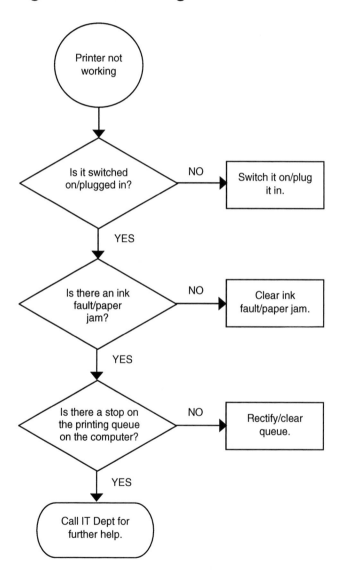

T&T No:	17		
Title:	FORCE FIELD ANALYSIS		
For use by:	Project Team Members or individuals wanting to increase chance of success		
When to use:	Goal setting or action planning		
Also see T&T No:	18, 20, 22, 23		
Difficulty Rating:	2	Category:	(C) Better Project Management

Force Field Analysis

What is it?

Force field analysis is a tool to increase the chance of successful achievement of a goal or action. It enables identification of the forces that will help or obstruct the initiation or maintenance of the desired change.

Force field analysis is a problem-solving technique which enables forward planning. It helps identify the forces which will have a positive helping effect, and those forces which will have a negative hindering effect. This enables assessment of the ease or difficulty which is likely to be encountered when implementing a desired change.

When to use it

When you think there is a need for change or improvement, force field analysis can be used to:

1. Identify the positive forces (actions) which will help you achieve your goal, and the negative forces which will get in the way of achieving your goal.
2. Assess the ease or difficulty of achieving the proposed change or improvement
3. Plan how to overcome the barriers to the proposed change or improvement.
4. Increase the chance of success by enhancing the positive factors.

Key steps

1. Define the problem : what is the current situation?
2. Define the objective : what is the aim or goal?
3. Prepare the force field diagram.
5. Identify the positive forces and represent them on the force field diagram.
6. Identify the negative forces and represent them on the force field diagram.
7. Analyse and evaluate which forces are open to change.
8. Rate each positive factor depending on the extent of the positive influence it may have. Identify ways of enhancing these.
9. Rate the negative hindering factors according to the ease which they may be weakened or eliminated. Identify ways of weakening them.
10. ✔ Produce an action plan to increase the likelihood of achieving your goal.

Stages 2, 4, 5, 7 and 8 relate directly to the **force field diagram**.

The force field diagram

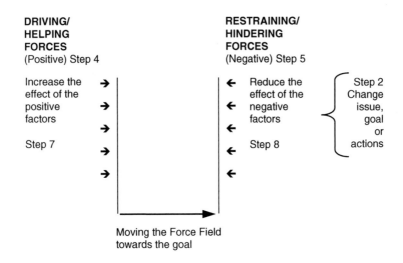

DRIVING/
HELPING
FORCES
(Positive) Step 4

RESTRAINING/
HINDERING
FORCES
(Negative) Step 5

Increase the → effect of the positive → factors →
Step 7 →
→

← Reduce the effect of the ← negative factors ←
Step 8 ←
←

Step 2
Change issue, goal or actions

Moving the Force Field towards the goal

Applying this tool to the production of this book, for example:

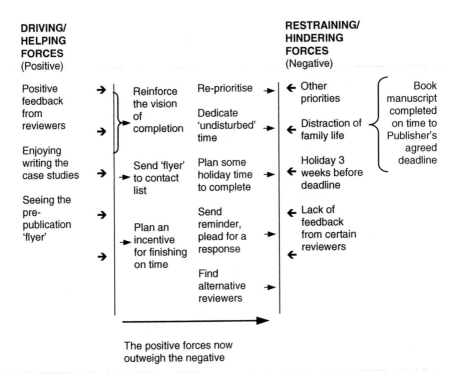

DRIVING/ HELPING FORCES (Positive)

RESTRAINING/ HINDERING FORCES (Negative)

Positive feedback from reviewers

→ Reinforce the vision of completion

Re-prioritise →

← Other priorities

Enjoying writing the case studies →

→ Send 'flyer' to contact list

Dedicate 'undisturbed' time →

← Distraction of family life

Seeing the pre-publication 'flyer' →

Plan some holiday time to complete →

Holiday 3 ← weeks before deadline

→ Plan an → incentive for finishing on time

Send reminder, plead for a response →

← Lack of feedback from certain ← reviewers

Find alternative reviewers →

Book manuscript completed on time to Publisher's agreed deadline

The positive forces now outweigh the negative

The above approach was originally described by Lewin, K., 1951.

T&T No:	18		
Title:	GOAL SETTING		
For use by:	All		
When to use:	To clarify targets		
Also see T&T No:	20, 22		
Difficulty Rating:	2	Category:	(C) Better Project Management

Goal Setting

The importance of goal setting

Managers should be able to help others set goals and apply the same discipline to themselves. Goal setting is important in managing performance and projects. Goals should focus on the WHAT to achieve, rather than the HOW to achieve.

Principles of goal setting

1. Goals stated in terms of accomplishments rather than behaviour.
2. Specific enough to drive action.
3. Goals that can be measured or verified.
4. Goals that are realistic.
5. Goals that address the problem they are trying to manage, or the level of improvement being aspired to.
6. Ensure that goals are owned and commitment to achieve them is given.
7. Goals are in keeping with the values of the individual and the organisation.
8. A realistic timeframe for accomplishment is determined.

Goals are statements that relate to achieving a desired future, examples of goal statements include:

- I will lose 20 pounds in weight in the next 3 months.

- I will increase my level of order completion by 10 more units per day with 99% accuracy in fulfilling customers' orders. This will be achieved by the end of this month.
- We will achieve a 20% increase in customer satisfaction rate by April 1st.
- We will reduce our costs by £5,000 on supplies by the year end.
- We will increase the capacity of space utilisation by 35% in 12 months.
- We will reduce the amount of adverse incident reporting by 25% in the next 3 months.

✍ Always state your goals in the 'positive' – avoid negative goals, such as:

- I will stop wasting my time dealing with meaningless emails.

It would be better to state:

- I will spend 25% less time a day dealing with emails, by the end of this week.

Don't be overwhelmed by goals. Better to have a vital few than a trivial many. Prioritise the most important to you.

Write your goals down and, if you can, communicate them to someone who is supportive.

You can use **SMARTER** goals as criteria for testing how robust and real they are.

Simple or Specific	Make sure the goals are understood, using clear language, avoiding vagueness and complexity
Measurable	There is a clear way of knowing if success has been achieved with specific outcomes. Questions to ask: how will you, and others, know you have achieved what you set out to achieve?
Acceptable	They are consistent with own and organisations values – i.e. it is important and worth the effort and resource investment.
Realistic	If it's too easy, you won't care to do it. If it's too hard, you won't dare to do it. Set goals that are stretching but attainable.

Time-framed   Set a time when you think the goal will be achieved. Mark important milestones to review progress.

Enthusiasm   Is the motivation and commitment there? Are the benefits explicit?

Resources   In terms of tangible (e.g. time or money) and intangible (e.g. own energy and support available).

T&T No:	19		
Title:	LINE GRAPHS		
For use by:	Anyone required to demonstrate factual change		
When to use:	Monitoring project progress or demonstrating trends		
Also see T&T No:	3, 20		
Difficulty Rating:	3	Category:	(C) Better Project Management

Line Graphs

What are they?

Line graphs are a common way of representing data in the form of a picture.

They show the direct relationships, for example, between two quantities at a glance.

When to use them

- Gathering data.
- Analysing data.
- Planning for implementing solutions.
- Implementing and testing solutions.
- Ensuring continuous improvement.

What do they achieve?

In the problem-solving process (see T&T No 20), it is often easier to see results when they are displayed on a graph than if the results were presented in the form of a table.

Seeing how variables have changed in the past can give a useful guide as to what can be expected in the future.

Line graphs compare two variables. Each variable is plotted along an axis. A line graph has a vertical axis and a horizontal axis. So, for example, if you wanted to graph the height of a ball after you have thrown it, you could put time along the horizontal, or x-axis, and height along the vertical, or y-axis.

Each type of graph has characteristics that make it useful in certain situations. Some of the strengths of line graphs are that:

- They are good at showing specific values of data, meaning that given one variable the other can easily be determined.
- They show trends in data clearly, meaning that they visibly show how one variable is affected by the other as it increases or decreases.
- They enable the viewer to make predictions about the results of data not yet recorded.

◀ Unfortunately, it is possible to alter the way a line graph appears to make data look a certain way. This is done by either not using consistent scales on the axes, meaning that the value in between each point along the axis may not be the same, or when comparing two graphs using different scales for each. It is important that we all be aware of how graphs can be made to look a certain way, when that might not be the way the data really is (see T&T No 3).

✔ As an exercise, gather the data related to customer complaints, adverse incidents or sickness rates. Track them over a period of two years. This may tell you if there are any seasonal variations or, with further enquiry, give an indication of significant influencing factors. This may then inform you of the direction to take to correct any adverse trends.

Case study: Line Graphs

Besides the presentation of factual data, line graphs can also be used to illustrate powerful concepts of personal growth and change.

Two I regularly use are:-

1. The S Curve and
2. The Change or Bereavement Curve

1. The S curve

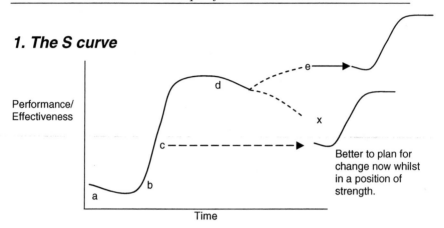

Performance/
Effectiveness

Time

Better to plan for
change now whilst
in a position of
strength.

Can be presented in terms of career or product life cycle.

a = start up, a lot to learn and develop, may be slow to get off the ground
b = steep learning curve, early results, growing confidence
c = competence realised, level of ability found. Ideally, this is the point when either a career change or a review of the market/product relationship should take place before:-
d = enthusiasm waning, career plateaux, moving towards choice time – retire or start a new S curve?

3. The change or bereavement curve

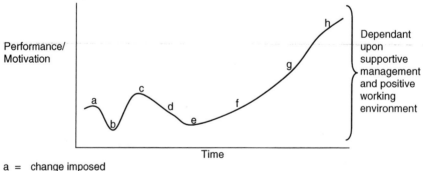

Performance/
Motivation

Time

Dependant
upon
supportive
management
and positive
working
environment

a = change imposed
b = shock
c = denial
d = realisation
e = depression
f = support for moving on, possibilities
g = new horizons
h = embracing change

T&T No:	20		
Title:	PROBLEM MANAGEMENT/SOLVING		
For use by:	All		
When to use:	Progressing change, improving situations		
Also see T&T No:	22, 23, 35		
Difficulty Rating:	4	Category:	(C) Better Project Management

Problem Management/Solving

What is it?

The problem-solving process is a logical sequence for solving problems and improving the quality of decisions.

When to use it

The problem-solving process can be applied to any problem situation and can also be used to tackle an opportunity for change or improvement.

What does it achieve?

Problems, no matter their size or complexity, can best be solved by proceeding through a sequence of steps. This ensures that everything possible will be done to apply the available resources in the most effective manner, to consider a number of options, and to select the best solution.

The problem-solving process can be used for:

- Producing a clear statement of the identified problem/opportunity.
- Gathering all necessary information associated with a problem/ opportunity.

- Analysing collected data and providing a clear statement of the root causes of a problem or the benefits of an opportunity.
- Clarifying what you are trying to achieve and set appropriate goals.
- Producing a list of all potential solutions to a problem/opportunity.
- Selecting the best solution to fit the problem/opportunity.
- Providing a plan for implementation.
- Implementing and testing a plan.
- Establishing a process for continuous improvement and holding the gains.

The three stages of managing change are consistent with effective problem-solving. These are:

   ⇨   What's going on now   (PRESENT)
   ⇨   What do we want 'it' to be   (FUTURE)
   ⇨   How are we going to achieve what we want   (ACTION)

✒ Applying this thinking to your projects to improve and other improvement initiatives will increase your chances of doing the right thing in the right way.

Be effective as well as efficient! Work Smarter!

(The following is based on the work of Professor Gerard Egan, 2002)

In summary, the key questions related to each stage are:

Present

Step 1   What's going on? (Data gathering)
Step 2   What's really going on? (Root causes)
Step 3   What, if tackled and put right, will have greatest effect? (Pareto)

Future

Step 4   What could/should it look like if resolved/changed?
Step 5   From Step 4 what are realistic goals?
Step 6   Are we committed to these goals?

Action

Step 7   How many ways can we think of to achieve these goals?
Step 8   Which ways are best?
Step 9   ✗ What's our detailed plan of action?

Case study: Problem Management/Solving

The three stages (present, future, action) and the nine questions within these three stages form the most powerful of all management tools. There is not a days' consultancy or managing within my own business where these questions aren't brought to life.

When I am invited to support or facilitate a meeting, I listen out for the type of language and decide whether it is the language of the present (i.e. 'the problem is...' or 'what's happening now is...'), the language of the future (i.e. 'we want...', 'we must achieve...', 'the quality required is...'), or the language of action (i.e. 'this is what we must do, how can we...')

If it is language of present, I ask – 'What's really going on, or what are you trying to achieve?'

If it is language of future, I ask – 'How many ways can you think of to get what you want, or what problems is this related to?'

If it is language of action, I ask – 'What is this trying to achieve?'

These questions offered by a manager or a facilitator, asked at the right time, can be a powerful way of bringing everyone to the same point and consolidating understanding of the agenda and direction.

T&T No:	21		
Title:	PROCESS ANALYSIS AND REDESIGN		
For use by:	Project Improvement Members		
When to use:	To improve efficiency		
Also see T&T No:	1, 14, 16, 17, 20, 24, 27, 40		
Difficulty Rating:	4	Category:	(C) Better Project Management

Process Analysis and Redesign

Aim

To review the efficiency of any process. It helps to create a detailed, sequential picture of a particular process, with all the steps clearly defined. This clarity allows problem identification and quality solutions to be arrived at within a given process (for example, cutting waiting time for treatment from 12 months to 18 weeks).

Using process analysis – an overview

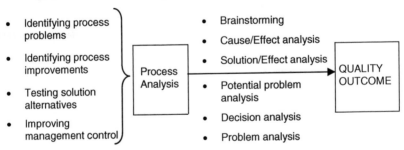

Process analysis – some definitions

Processes ...are SPECIFIC FUNCTIONS that make up the total business or management activity. Examples include standard setting, managing a budget or recruiting new staff.

Tasks …are the lowest operation levels within processes. A process is a series of interrelated tasks. Examples would be arranging meeting times, or writing a job description.

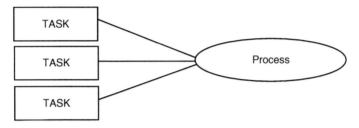

♦✳ Requirement for effective process

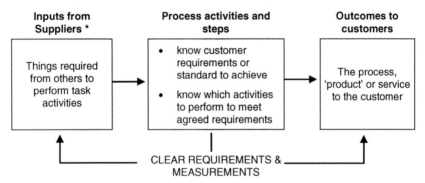

* = Suppliers and Customers can be internal or external (see T&T No 27).

◀ฺ) Rules for process analysis

- Agree, define and review measurable customer requirements.
- Clearly define and delineate the process.
- Each task of process analysis must have an owner.
- Clearly establish task boundaries.
- Agree inputs and outputs for each task.
- Ensure all process tasks are identified and agreed.
- Build control points and performance measurements into the process.
- Clearly establish the interfaces that exist between the process under scrutiny and others within the organisation – how does one impact the other?

87

Process analysis – Outline of the 9 steps

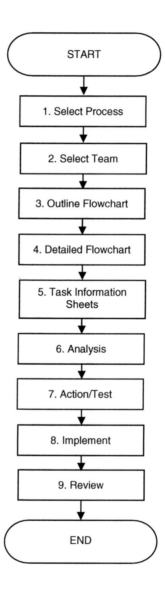

START

1. Select Process

2. Select Team

3. Outline Flowchart

4. Detailed Flowchart

5. Task Information Sheets

6. Analysis

7. Action/Test

8. Implement

9. Review

END

1. Select the process

Based on:-
* own knowledge
* audit
* reports
* research
* staff reporting
* financial/statistics
* other agreed criteria.

2. Select the team ♔

* Team leader – should ideally be the 'owner' of the process. Otherwise, it should be the person with the highest dependency on the process – i.e. the person most accountable for its success.
* Team members – individuals with experience and knowledge of process steps. Both users and designers.
* The first task of the leader is to ensure that all team members understand the purpose and methods of process analysis.

3. Outline flowchart (see T&T No 16) ☐

* Captures the major tasks involved in a process and illustrates their relationship to each other.
* Should be produced by the team, reaching agreement over each point.
* Use 'post-its' to write key steps on. These can then easily be shuffled around until consensus is reached.
* Utilise whiteboards/Nobo boards/flipcharts to ensure everyone can see.
* Produce the final chart using the standard symbols below. Appropriate use of these is shown in the outline of the nine steps seen later.

Process analysis – Steps 1 to 3

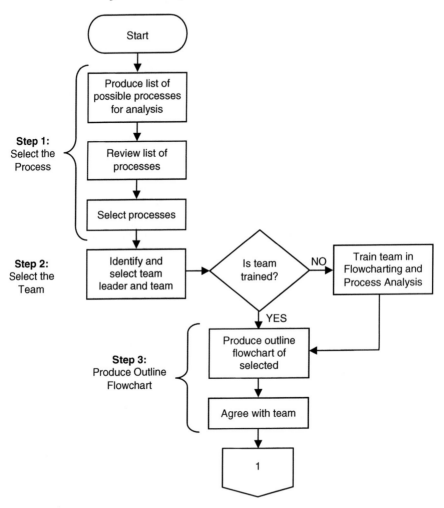

4. Detailed flowcharts

- Move from identifying major steps to detailing all tasks within a process.
- Identify all:-
    - Inputs
    - Outputs
    - Routines
    - Procedures
    - Negotiables
    - Non-negotiables
    - Duplications
    - Dead-ends
    - Inconsistencies
    - Gaps.
- ☐ Each team member may develop detailed flowchart for their task area within the process, and then present it to the whole team for awareness, agreement and discussion.

Process analysis – Step 4
Detailed flowchart creation

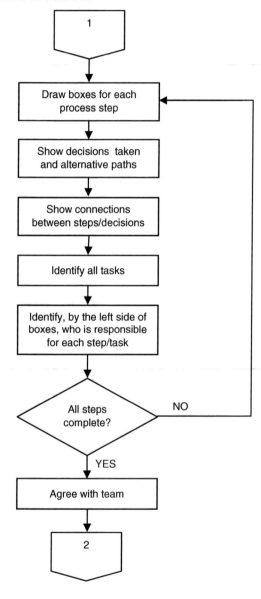

5. Task information sheets

- The purpose of task information sheets is to link the detailed process flow with existing written procedures, controls and systems.
- This task will highlight where these do not exist!
- When a process is to be changed, the appropriate task information sheet can be used to identify which procedures, controls and systems will need to be changed.
- The following details will need to be recorded:-
  i. PROCESS – name of process in which the task is being carried out.
  ii. TASK DESCRIPTION – brief statement of task. Note whether it is manual or automatic.
  iii. TASK NUMBER – unique reference number for each task in the process.
  iv. OWNER – name of task owner.
  v. DEPARTMENT – owner's department.
  vi. SKILLS REQUIRED – brief inventory of skill(s) required to carry out the task.
  vii. MEDIA USED – if appropriate (e.g. paper, magnetic disc, etc.).
  viii. STANDARD DOCUMENTS – list those used (e.g. history sheet, pathology forms, wage slips, etc.).
  ix. MEASUREMENTS IN PLACE – standard performance indicators allocated to the task.
  x. EXCEPTION CONTROL PROCEDURES – how are problems in the process reported, and to whom?
  xi. DEPENDENT TASKS – brief outline of any tasks dependent on this one.
  xii. OBSERVED PROBLEMS/OPPORTUNITIES – brief description of deficiencies found and ideas for improvement.
  xiii. POSSIBLE ACTION – list ideas for action to improve the task. They can be picked up in Stage 6 – Analysis.

6. Analysis

- This is achieved by carefully scrutinising the flowcharts and task information sheets, and identifying opportunities and areas for development.
- Use the criteria in Stage 4, and also check:-
  - Is the process description complete?

- Are there any dead-ends?
- Are parts of the process duplicated?
- Are parts of the process not needed?
- Are there gaps in the process?
- Are there procedures missing?
- Is there a method for detecting and reporting process inconsistencies?
- Are responsibilities split for simple tasks?
- Are relevant measures in place?
- NB: Cause and effect diagrams and Problem analysis will help identify root causes of problems. (See T&T No 1 and 20.)
- Simple problems can be quickly fixed, but larger difficulties are considered in Section 7.

7. *Action planning*

- Look at each identified opportunity/problem in turn.
- Use action planning. (See T&T No 14.)
- Other tools and techniques to help the process include:-
  - Brainstorming. (See T&T No 40.)
  - Solution effect analysis. (See T&T No 24.)
  - Force field analysis. (See T&T No 17.)
- ᛟᛟᛟ Use the group to generate agreed, step by step strategies for action.

Process analysis – Steps 5, 6 and 7

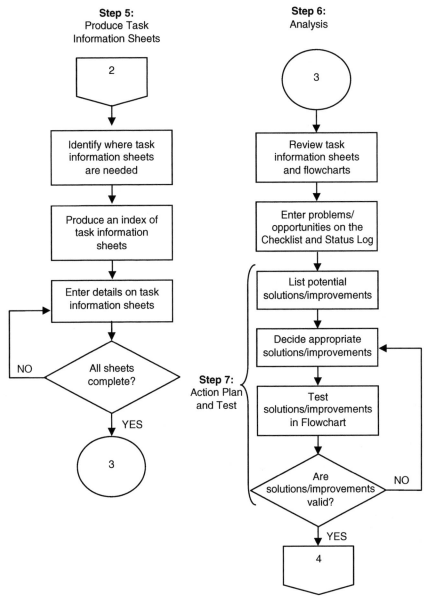

Step 5:
Produce Task
Information Sheets

Step 6:
Analysis

2

3

Identify where task
information sheets
are needed

Review task
information sheets
and flowcharts

Produce an index of
task information
sheets

Enter problems/
opportunities on the
Checklist and Status Log

Enter details on task
information sheets

List potential
solutions/improvements

Decide appropriate
solutions/improvements

NO

All sheets
complete?

Step 7:
Action Plan
and Test

Test
solutions/improvements
in Flowchart

YES

3

Are
solutions/improvements
valid?

NO

YES

4

8. Implementation

- The group members now need to communicate the improvements or new processes to the wider workforce.
- For each task improvement, carry out the change and measure the effect. Examine the overall effects on the process as a whole. Note positive and adverse effects.
- If improvements do not work, return to the action plan and agree an alternative with the team.
- The conclusion of this step occurs when task improvements are successfully included with no adverse effects on the process as a whole.

9. Review

- Establish regular, timed review dates to ensure that new task improvements continue to be carried out.
- If not, return to either Section 3 and 4, or 7 – to establish alternatives for action with the team's agreement.

Process analysis – Steps 8 and 9
Implementation and Review

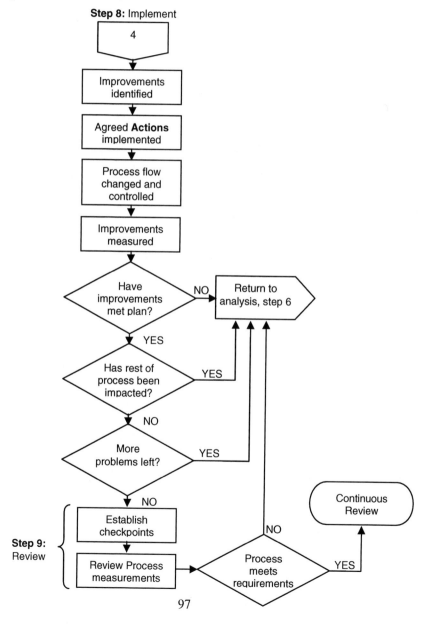

Step 8: Implement

4

Improvements identified

Agreed **Actions** implemented

Process flow changed and controlled

Improvements measured

Have improvements met plan?

NO → Return to analysis, step 6

YES

Has rest of process been impacted?

YES

NO

More problems left?

YES

NO

Step 9:
Review

Establish checkpoints

Review Process measurements

Process meets requirements

NO

YES

Continuous Review

Case study: Process Analysis and Redesign

In a small acute hospital someone asked the question: why does it take a week to get the result of certain blood tests when the actual test takes less than 30 minutes to set up and 12 hours to get the result?

This was an important question as some of these tests/results were key factors in deciding whether a patient should be discharged or not. Patients were waiting in a hospital bed for up to a week, at great expense, for results that, in theory, should be delivered within 24 hours.

A small team conducted a process analysis which consisted of physically following and tracking each event, from blood test request to blood results given.

These were some of the events:-

- Blood test request – left in the request tray waiting for the morning round of phlebotomy (blood taken).
- Blood taken and specimen left at collection point.
- Porter collects specimen.
- Specimen left in receiver fridge in Pathology Department.
- Specimen taken out – tested.
- Results recorded – written up – left in results tray for porter collection.
- Porter collects and delivers to Ward.
- Results inputted into Case Notes.
- Results reviewed by Doctor on next ward round.

At each point, there was a potential waiting time of up to ½ a day.

Once this was realised, a small multi-disciplinary team which included the head porter, pathologist, ward clerk, nurse, registrar and hospital manager – came together to redesign the blood requisition and results service.

This involved everyone incorporating new ways of working – but in the end, significant savings were made in terms of less bed days as results were turned around within 24 hours.

zT&T No:	22
Title:	PROJECT WAY OF WORKING
For use by:	Project Team Members
When to use:	To progress or review projects
Also see T&T No:	20, 23, 33

Difficulty Rating:	4	Category:	(C) Better Project Management

Project Way of Working

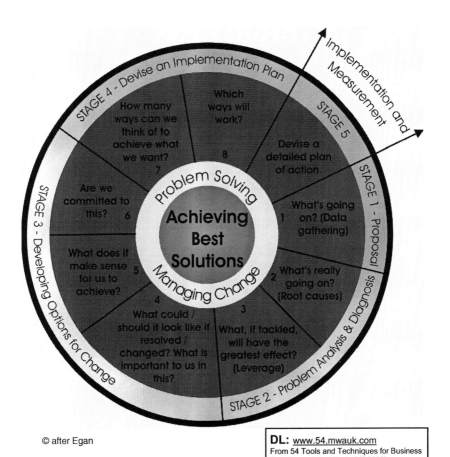

© after Egan

DL: www.54.mwauk.com
From 54 Tools and Techniques for Business Excellence, Mike Wash (MB2000)

What is a project?

A project can be any proposal to change something or implement something new that will require staff, customers or suppliers to behave or react differently, such as order processing, newsletter, spares access, policy for discount, moving office, and so on.

5-stage project management

Stage one: Establishing the project

The first stage is to ensure that the project is set up to succeed. Likely tasks within this stage would be:-

- Agreeing project purpose.
- Establishing sponsorship arrangements.
- Recruiting project leader. (Someone who would lead the project as part of their day to day job – not a full time or specialist role.)
- Recruiting project team from the key stakeholders. Agreeing roles and responsibilities.
- Agreeing project stages, timescales, discussing project tools including systems of measurement.
- Ensuring the provision of any skills training that may be required by members of the project team.

This first stage is critical to ensure the success of the project. Clear project purpose and clear management arrangements should together provide the necessary direction.

These can be summarised on a project proposal form, designed to help consistency of approach and communication (see example form on page 101).

Stage one – Step one

Maximise our knowledge of the present situation. (**Step 1**)

What's going on? Whatever the proposal, whether it's problem orientated (e.g. 'we need to improve the way we communicate with our customer') or connected with new implementation of a policy or system, the first stage is to complete a proposal and gather initial information about the current situation. (See example form on page 101.)

Example Form   Project Proposal

Identification Name _____

Start Date _____

1. Initial presentation or awareness of need for change.

2. Project Sponsor _____

3. Project Leader _____

4. Project Team _____

5. Initial intended outcome (to be reviewed when clear vision and goals are set)

6. Approximate timescale (to be reviewed when project scope is more definite)

7. Expected benefits

8. Initial estimate of costs and/or savings

9. Risks (Reviewing potential pitfalls and if necessary design contingency plans, see T&T No 33)

10. Key stakeholders to be included in the communication plan. Description of first steps in the communication plan. What, to whom, when and how?

DL: www.54.mwauk.com
From 54 Tools and Techniques for Business Excellence, Mike Wash (MB2000)

Project roles and responsibilities

Each project will require leadership, management and a range of experts dependent on the needs of particular projects. As a minimum, projects should have an identified project sponsor and a project leader. There are also other roles that may be necessary but should not be obligatory.

Project sponsor

The Project sponsor will be a senior manager who is best placed to champion the project. They may or may not have identified the need for the project but will certainly be very keen that the project succeeds. The project sponsor will play a lead role in conceiving and scoping the project but will be removed from planning and implementation. The project sponsor is likely to be involved in unblocking projects, supporting the management of resistance and keeping a watchful eye on progress. They will probably attend the occasional meeting of the project team but can expect regular briefings.

Project leader

The Project leader will have day to day responsibility for the project. Their role will be to lead the project team through the five stages of project management, described within this T&T. The project leader is likely to bring in general change management and team leadership skills rather than technical skills. The project leader will report to the project sponsor for the purposes of the project.

Other roles

There may be many other possible roles which would relate to specific needs of the project. These 'experts' would be called upon as appropriate and may be able to offer skills associated with database management, process mapping, costing quality, information recording, meeting organisation and administration.

Project team

The project team will be formed by the project leader. It will be lead by the project leader and will comprise of individuals who can contribute to the project, either because of their knowledge of the subject area or because they possess relevant skills. The role of the project team will be to play a full and equitable role in the five stages of project management.

Other groups

The project team may wish to establish other groups to help with particular aspects of the project. For example, to assist with diagnosis and understanding customer needs or to assist with aspects of implementation.

A project communications plan

A project communications plan is a critical element for securing successful projects. The purpose of a communication plan for a project is to ensure there are no surprises – so that everyone likely to be effected by the proposed change is informed at each milestone and involved/consulted appropriately.
This will minimise the likelihood of confusion and resistance.

Stage two

♦ Personal experiences of working within this framework as a whole have been good. However, stage two is a point at which the process can become stalled as people search for the 'Holy Grail' of right data, right answers and invariably keep on searching. This can be a very de-motivating experience and lead to a loss in momentum.

It may be worth stating that these stages need fixed time limits if the project is to succeed. The concept of information being 'good enough' is important particularly when dealing with clinicians, scientists or academics of any sort.

Making an informed change and being prepared to go round the wheel again and fine-tune the decision is all part of a learning approach and more importantly, gets on with the progress of behaviour and system change.

Processes that stall because of a perceived lack of adequate information are susceptible to sabotage and delaying tactics. In the end, a further bit of information may be inconsequential to the final outcome and may cost the organisation dear in terms of lost momentum, slow change and competitive advantage.

It may be worth reflecting on the Apollo space missions which averaged only 3% of time as directly on course – the rest was all fine tuning in Houston!

Problem analysis and diagnosis

The purpose of the second stage is to develop a shared and educated understanding of the nature of the problem and how things work at present. Project management helps us to:

- Find the root causes of problems and consider causes that may have been hidden from us. **(Step 2)**
- Prioritise further consideration of those aspects of a problem that, if tackled, will lead to the greatest leverage to make a qualitative difference. **(Step 3)**

Stage three: Developing options for change

The purpose of this third stage is to ensure that any change is prompted by a vision. Project management should not just be about solving problems, but it should capitalise on the opportunity to provide the optimum service or product. Likely tasks within this stage would be:

- Developing a vision of what the ideal service or product might look like. **(Step 4)**
- Understanding explicitly customer (*) needs.
- Considering scenarios in terms of maximising efficiency, meeting customer needs, managing staff concerns and considering organisational practicality.
- Setting short-term, medium-term and long-term goals that can assist the realistic progression towards a vision. **(Step 5)**
- Using customer* feedback to test the viability of the vision.
- Gaining commitment to the vision from those affected by it. **(Step 6)**

* Customer: *definition* – anyone on the receiving end of a service. These can be internal, such as HR providing recruitment support, or external.

Stage Four: Devise an implementation plan

The purpose of this fourth stage is to agree a plan for realising the vision and effecting change. Likely tasks within this stage would be:

- Thinking creatively to discover all the possible options and resources for delivering the agreed vision. **(Step 7)**
- Agreeing on the best fit. **(Step 8)**
- Agreeing the establishment of a measuring and monitoring system. **(Step 9)**

- Developing a critical path or change management plan for action and implementation. (**Step 9**)
- Ensuring resources and their efficient use.
- Briefing and reassuring staff.
- Analysing and managing resistance.
- Meeting staff training needs.

Stage Five: Implementation, measurement and review

The purpose of this fifth and final stage is to address issues of implementation, measurement and review. Implementation should come relatively easy if the previous stages have been tackled properly. Measurement should not simply be a bureaucratic exercise but more a tool by which success can be demonstrated and learning opportunities highlighted. Likely tasks within this stage would be:

- Monitoring implementation. (**Step 9** onwards)
- Measuring outcomes – qualitatively and quantitatively.
- Reviewing and then making adjustments.
- Communicating learning, success, progress and enthusiasm.
- Proving support to staff and others affected by change.
- Consolidating gains.
- Standing down the project team. (An implementation team may be needed which may involve some members of the original project team, but will likely need other members with different skill sets and interests.)

Case study: Project Way of Working

An example of a completed proposal form is given below. It is from a wastewater company who were in the middle of a company wide development programme. This particular project resulted in all projects managed using a similar process and enabled new changes to be incorporated quickly and efficiently.

Project Proposal

Identification Name   Project Way of Working (PWOW)

Start Date   01/06/06

1. **The need for change.**
   During the Management Development Programme (MDP) our group agreed that a cultural change was needed primarily to facilitate projects to be completed. It was agreed that there was no formal structure to enable projects to be completed and after a short period they lost focus and fizzled out. This model would be a useful induction tool for new employees. The recent completion of the MDP also provided a healthy climate to introduce this way of working and gain a buy in from all managers.

2. **Project Sponsor**   Craig Brighouse

3. **Project Leader**   Gavin Leeman

4. **Project Team**   Gavin Leeman, Niall Jones, more members required

5. **Intended outcome**
   This will quite simply be a uniform, company wide model for all projects. This model will be retained on the Intranet in the form of a written procedure and flowchart.

6. **Timescale**
   To be completed by the end of 2006.

7. **Expected benefits**
   - Uniform way of working with projects throughout the company.
   - Projects will be seen right through to completion.
   - The generation of more revenue by efficiency savings.
   - It is a good communication vehicle and will assist the Communication project.
   - It will build a team culture.
   - It will aid personal development.
   - It allows visibility of project progress.
   - It embeds change.
   - It is a good quality tool.
   - It will be a historical record of achievement, something that we can later refer to as a reference.

8. Estimate of costs/savings

There are lost opportunity costs (salary costs of those working on the project) that are difficult to equate. I would envisage maybe 10 hours (each member) being sufficient to complete the procedure and flowchart.

It has been widely known that as a company we have historically been good with ideas but poor at implementing them. Savings will be made company wide due to:-

- The increased efficiency coming from project completions.
- Freeing up more time to do more value adding work.
- Getting it right first time
- Less staff turnover.

9. Risks

The main risks that have been identified are i) We lose the momentum gained from the MDP and this key project fails to deliver as planned, ii) The new Managing Director doesn't want to work this way and iii) a key member of the team leaves.

10. Key stakeholders

The project sponsor, Team Members, those that the project impacts upon (internal customers, external customers and suppliers), Corporate HQ and our own staff.

Gavin Leeman, Manufacturing/QHSE Manager
11/07/2006

T&T No:	23		
Title:	PROJECT CONTROL – STEP BY STEP, MEETING BY MEETING		
For use by:	Project Leaders, Chairs of Project Meetings		
When to use:	Moving projects on		
Also see T&T No:	22		
Difficulty Rating:	3	Category:	(C) Better Project Management

Project Control – Step by Step, Meeting by Meeting

Based on Project Way of Working (see T&T No 22)

1st meeting   *Stage 1 Step 1*

- ☛ Set the climate:
  - – Make introductions; help reduce anxiety levels.
  - – Set standards and ground rules.
- Clarify roles.
- Explain the approach.
- Introduce the project proposal. (Refer to example form within Project Way of Working, T&T No 22.)
- Use brainstorming to share perceptions of the current situation.
- Use the proposal form to guide discussion around the Project.
- Agree actions before next meeting (e.g. informal data gathering and communication).

2nd meeting   *Stage 2 Steps 2 and 3*

- Feedback on acceptance of proposal from the senior manager or sponsor.
- ◀ Further input of any new information is offered following informal data gathering.

- Agreement as to the approach to data gathering and action as to who's doing what between now and next meeting.
- Agree basic agenda for next meeting re presentation of data.

3rd meeting   *Stage 2 Steps 2 and 3*

- Present findings from data gathering.
- ⚕ Agree   root causes ⎤
                   priority issues ⎬ as appropriate.
                   leverage points ⎦
- Agree further actions to validate findings.

Stage 3 Step 4

- ⬚ Brainstorm preferred outcome relevant to the above (Vision building).
- Agree to shape the brainstorm into a 'Vision' statement for next meeting.
- Agree communication/consultation actions.

4th meeting   *Stage 3 Step 4, 5 and 6*

- Present project 'Vision'
- Gain reaction, feedback and adjust accordingly.
- Agree major 'goals'.
- ◁⫶ Test Commitment.

Stage 4 Step 7

- Brainstorm action to achieve goals.

Stage 4 Step 8

- ✒ Agree process for putting together an action plan.

5th meeting   *Stage 4 Step 9*

- Present proposal action plan (build up a critical path).
- ☞ Agree first steps.
- Present critical path to steering group.

6th meeting   *Stage 5*

- Agree implementation process. (May require a new team.)
- ✗ Implement.

7th meeting

- Review success of first steps.
- Agree monitoring and reporting process.

T&T No:	24		
Title:	SOLUTION EFFECT ANALYSIS		
For use by:	Project Team Members		
When to use:	Test out viability or impact of change		
Also see T&T No:	1, 40		
Difficulty Rating:	2	Category:	(C) Better Project Management

Solution Effect Analysis

What is it?

Solution effect analysis is a technique which may be used in improvement projects or problem situations to identify how different possible solutions will affect an organisation/department if implemented.

It makes use of a simple diagram which, can be used in a variety of ways by a group or an individual.

When might it be used?

- Solution effect analysis is an invaluable aid in the later stages of project management. It can also be used to test out assumptions made when a particular solution is put forward.
- It is a useful aid to problem management in general.
- It is a useful means to getting a quality improvement group working together in its early history.

Benefits of using solution effect analysis

- As well as identifying individual effects of solutions, groups of effects can be located that are not immediately obvious.
- Use of the technique in a group enables everyone to contribute. In this way, the widest range of expertise can be drawn on.

Developing the solution effect diagram
☐ + ﬗ

1. Establish the solution to be investigated.
2. On the flipchart, or paper, draw a box with the solution statement in it.
3. Draw a line extending from the right of the box.
4. Identify the main categories of effects (e.g. manpower, machinery, methods, materials). Develop categories that suit your business.
5. Draw lines extending from the one attached to the box, one for each category.
6. Brainstorm (see T&T No 40) for sub-effects in each category, attaching them to the appropriate line. (This can be done using post-its, attaching them to a flipchart or board, and moving them as the group considers where the effects should lie).
7. Once the effects are located, lines expressing relationships between the effects can be added, usually in a different colour.

Example of a solution effect diagram

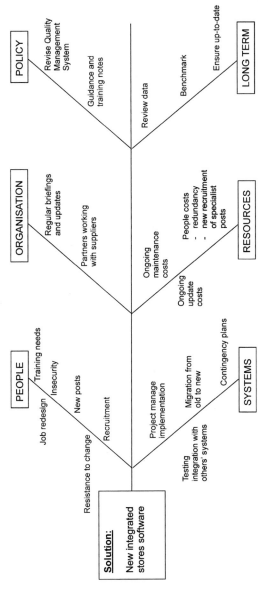

T&T No:	25		
Title:	BENCHMARKING		
For use by:	Senior Managers, Project Leaders, Department Heads, Specialist Heads		
When to use:	To find out how well you are really doing compared to others		
Also see T&T No:	21		
Difficulty Rating:	4	Category:	(D) Being the Best – Quality and Excellence

Benchmarking

What is benchmarking?

Comparing yourself with other organisations, that has similar products, services or processes, and then learning from these companies or organisations. Optimum learning comes from comparing yourself with market leaders or your toughest competitor.

Why benchmarking?

How do you know you are performing well? Do you want to know how you compare with others in your industry? Do you want to learn from others approaches to customer satisfaction and process efficiency outside your industry? Benchmarking is a start to comparing yourself with 'best in class' performers. It involves understanding the differences between you and others then learning from each other (easier if not competitors) to optimise performance.

Five steps to make benchmarking work

1. Determine what to benchmark

Decide the critical performance factors at which you want to excel. Popular issues include customer satisfaction rating and feedback process, speed of production and/or delivery, complaints, sickness rates, staff surveys and process efficiency.

2. Understand the internal processes

✦ Using the *outputs** that you have decided to measure, identify the business processes which contribute to them. Define the processes using flowcharts and determine the measures which are true indicators of performance.

Using a process map (see T&T No 21) tracking every interaction from start to finish can, in itself, give an indication of how efficient you are.

*Outputs are indicators giving you a 'quality' measure. This can be in terms of efficiency (i.e. best result within resources allocated) and/or effectiveness (e.g. customer or staff satisfaction).

3. Identify the best of the best

Compare: other sites/departments – competitors – the best firms in similar fields – the best across industry groupings.

There are benchmarking groups, associations and networks that exist and are all geared to helping cross-organisational quality improvement.

4. Evaluate the benchmarked group

Analyse the data, seeking to excel against each criterion. ✦ Often best done with mutual agreement, shared visits and discussions.

5. Get people involved

Commit yourself to use results. Communicate the opportunities to those who can act. Assign responsibility for key improvement areas. Start a planned improvement process. Agree when and how to repeat the comparison. How do you know things have improved unless you measure them?

Case study

The Royal Liverpool Children's Hospital, Alder Hey, was about to embark upon a total organisation change process. They wanted to learn and find out how their plans, designs and processes compared with other organisations further down this journey of change.

A community hospital trust in Scotland had been three years into a similar process, and their Chief Executive and Finance Director agreed to present an overview of what they had achieved so far.

Following the presentation, a team of managers from the Children's Hospital went on a fact finding visit to the Scottish Hospital and through this visit, comparison and lessons learnt were fed back and influenced design and emphasis regarding organisation development.

Alder Hey managers continue to benchmark through a process they call 'Team Raiding' – visiting different organisations who seem to be the 'Best in Class' at what they do – to find out specifics.

This needs preparation and organisation, but can be one of the best ways of getting to the heart of things and seeing how things do get done differently and with good results. Addenbrooks Hospital, Cambridge, recently had their top team visit Alder Hey for these exact reasons – both organisations got a lot out of the visit.

◄» Organisations sometimes work too long in isolation. They can lose sight of how the market is changing or how competitors are developing (eg Marks and Spencer and IBM have, in the past, made this mistake). It is therefore important that an external view is taken from time to time and a trip to another business can be valuable time out. These learning exchanges can develop into effective, mutually enhancing strategic partnerships.

There are many resources available to support and encourage Benchmarking. See www.constructingexcellence.org.uk as one example of a site offering benchmarking opportunities.

T&T No:	26		
Title:	COST OF QUALITY		
For use by:	Supervisors, Managers, Trainers		
When to use:	When failure becomes an issue		
Also see T&T No:	13, 15, 21, 27, 40		
Difficulty Rating:	2	Category:	(D) Being the Best – Quality and Excellence

Cost of Quality

What is it?

The price of non-conformance (Crosby, P.) or the cost of poor quality (Juran, J.), the term 'cost of quality' refers to the costs associated with providing poor quality product or service.

These costs are usually conceptualised under three categories:

1. Prevention costs.
2. Failure costs.
3. Appraisal costs.

1. Prevention costs

These are all the costs associated with the time and resources directed towards getting the quality right first time. This is the investment put into preventing mistakes or substandard products and service.

Examples:

- Mission, role, clear customer requirements, objectives, training, education.
- Reviews, to learn how to improve. Effective problem-solving.
- Forward planning, clear priorities, accurate forecasts and resource allocation.

2. Failure costs

Costs associated with having to put things right that should not have occurred in the first place. These are all the additional resources needed to recover from mistakes, faults, defects and substandard products or service.

Examples:
- Chasing reports, notes or results.
- Misreading data.
- Slow transport system – internal mail.
- Meetings starting and finishing late.
- System failure.
- Inadequate or inappropriate training.

(For further examples, please see case study.)

3. Appraisal costs

These are all the costs associated with the time and resources invested in systems and procedures to check that the quality of the product or service meets a standard set either by the company or an external auditing body.

Examples
- Monitoring, evaluating, checking against standards.
- Proof reading.
- Audits and inspection.
- Check lists indicating fulfilment of contract.
- Appraisals if measured against competencies or standards/norms.

Managing the cost of quality

☛ Reducing the cost of quality is the principal target in organisation improvement.

Reduction in failure costs and the gradual decrease in the need to rely on heavy appraisal costs constitute some of the most significant financial impact on improvement. A small increase in prevention costs can create a massive reduction in failure costs. See diagram on page 123.

The success of quality cost containment relies on each individual within the organisation being fully aware of the impact s/he has on the customer/supplier chain, and how the effect of sub-standard work reverberates around the chain, incurring obvious and less obvious costs as time and materials are wasted, work patterns are disrupted, and re-work is undertaken.

The key to understanding the above is clear knowledge of who the customer is, both externally and internally, and aiming to exceed their expectation by delivering this excellence.

The development of this knowledge implies increased communication and cross functional problem-solving, which includes customer and supplier.

Each person, then, must develop a concern for excellence, and constantly strive for 'right first time, every time'. To do this, individual effort in this direction must be given adequate recognition, opportunity and authority to change systems etc.

Identifying who constitutes customer and supplier is not always easy in a large organisation. To illustrate this, try the following exercise:

Identifying internal customers and suppliers
(See T&T No 27.)

1. ☐ Take a large sheet of paper, and brainstorm everybody and department whose activity impinges on your ability to deliver a quality product or service, and whose ability to deliver quality depends on the quality of your work.
2. Now link them, on a separate sheet, trying to illustrate the relationships and dependencies between the beginning and the end of the process.
3. To make the exercise easier (!) divide the customers and suppliers into internal and external. Or try major customers/suppliers and stakeholders (those who have an interest in or are directly affected by the quality of your work).
4. If you do this as a group exercise, it may be useful to use 'Post-it notes', with the various persons or departments written on them, and then the group can try different combinations until agreement is reached.
5. This will produce a complex picture of a relationship network – next steps involve identifying the critical connections and improving them.

Identifying quality costs

1. ⛹ Brainstorm a list of your department's major products and services.
2. For each one, list the activities that actually take place in the delivery of each one.
3. Using the prevention, failure and appraisal criteria, identify each activity as a quality cost. For failure costs, note down preventative activity that could be explored. For appraisal activity, note down measures that could be explored to reduce the need for appraisal.
4. Finish with a general discussion of how quality costs and the nature of the customer/supplier chain may affect each other, and how it could look if done differently.

Case Study 1: Cost of Quality – Prevention, Appraisal and Failure

A large law firm decided to bring all their staff together to identify how they could improve their practice. The concepts of 'Cost of Quality' were introduced and the rules of brainstorming explained.

Below is the output of their identified failure costs:-

GROUPWORK: THE COST OF QUALITY 'What wastes your time?'

Delay
Ineffective internal procedures
Lack of resource
Lack of quality of decision-making
Referrals to the complaints department
Appeals
Failure to anticipate strategic changes
Inconsistency
Panic
Lack of effective planning time
Perceived lack of confidence in staff inhibits risk taking
Time wasted in meetings
Time wasted chasing Help Desk
System crashing
Inadequate financial information
Inefficient decision-making process
Unclear structure for decision-making
Inadequate managers – inconsistent
Weak management culture

Inconsistent policy
Lack of direction and focus
Governance – interference of Office holders/Council in management
Bureaucracy
Getting things done
Poor support – IT/telephone/printers etc
Poor Communication

SUMMARISED – CRITICAL COSTS

Inefficiency of internal procedures	
Poor decision-making process	3 votes
Failure to anticipate strategic change	
Weak management culture	3 votes
Lack of direction and focus	2 votes
Governance	1 vote

From this list, the Pareto items (see T&T No 13) were identified and project teams were formed to further explore what was going on, what should be in place and the action required to improve. The project teams were focused around the following:-
1. Inefficiency of internal procedures and poor decision-making process
2. Failure to anticipate strategic change, lack of direction and focus
3. Weak governance

Case Study 2:   Manny's – Auditing, Wasting and Customer Experience

'Manny's' is a restaurant offering popular dishes from steak to fish. It is situated in Haines City near Kissimmee, Florida. The business is run by a Greek family. 'Manny' bought it on first viewing, as he had a clear vision and immediately recognised its potential. It is open seven days a week, and every evening it is full from 3.30pm to 10.00pm. Manny was keen to encourage and teach his son (Nikko) the important basics of running a restaurant. Shortly after opening, one of the first jobs he gave to his son was to work in the kitchen, and to monitor what goes into the waste bin. (Appraisal activity/cost). Every server who cleared the table brought the customers 'leftovers' to the waste bin. Nikko's job was to go back to the customer, whose leftovers were more than a mouthful, and ask 'WHY WASN'T IT GOOD ENOUGH TO TAKE HOME?' (A wonderful quality catch phrase and a great way of keeping in touch with what customers really think.)

Case Study 3: Failure Costs Justify Investment

Whilst doing an audit in a telecommunications company, we discovered that the telephone engineers repairing and installing phones for residential customers were very dissatisfied with the stores systems. Each individual engineer was unhappy with collecting orders for the day from the central stores, visiting customers and discovering that there was equipment missing or wrong. This is why they began to build their own equipment stores in each corner of the yard, and in each van. Over the year, each engineer began to put their customer's orders right from their own stores.

This eventually lead to excess accumulation of out of date stock. However, it fuelled a thriving private business for the engineers – supplying friends and neighbours with phones and extensions, etc. The cost of failure due to a poor central stores system was approximated in the millions of pounds range.

The audit became part of a strong business case for a completely new stores ordering and allocation system. (This case study is also presented to illustrate Cost Benefit Analysis. See T&T No 15)

Case study 4: Disney Reputation Saved (Failure Into Prevention)

In my excitement at arriving at one of the Disney Golf courses in Orlando, Florida; I forgot my golf glove. So, I decided to treat myself to a Disney glove. Imagine my disappointment when, having tried on a glove and realising it wasn't my size and that I needed the next size – i.e. medium and they hadn't got any in stock!

Disney had run out of Medium sized golf gloves! (Failure cost = loss of sale and customer disappointment). I decided to play without a glove. As I approached the tee to prepare to take my shot, the server from the shop ran up and said 'Sir, we apologise for not having the right size golf glove for you, will you accept the one you tried on earlier as a gift from us? I know it's a little bit big, but it may help.'

Failure turned to prevention – customer happy, Disney reputation saved!

Cost of quality diagram

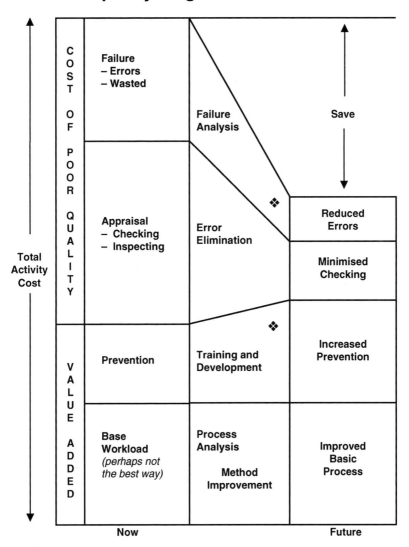

❖ = Small increase in prevention costs can have a direct impact on significantly reducing failure costs.

DL: www.54.mwauk.com
From 54 Tools and Techniques for Business Excellence, Mike Wash (MB2000)

T&T No:	27		
Title:	CUSTOMER/SUPPLIER RELATIONSHIPS (INTERNAL)		
For use by:	Supervisors, Team Leaders, Facilitators		
When to use:	To improve internal relationships between departments		
Also see T&T No:	6, 12, 34		
Difficulty Rating:	2	Category:	(D) Being the Best – Quality and Excellence

Customer/Supplier Relationships (Internal)

The matrix structure of internal customer/supplier relationships within a team or tier of management can be represented as follows:

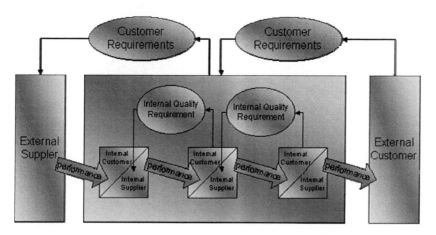

What is it?

♦* This is a technique used to identify the inter-dependencies of individuals and teams within an organisation. It reinforces the importance of communication, responsiveness and respect across all departments.

- List the people in your team.
- List the people in other departments that you are dependant upon for either information or understanding.
- For each one identify the key requirement you have of each other to achieve your objectives.
- Identify those whom you are in partnership with to achieve certain objectives.

☐ Draw your structure map

a) Place yourself at the centre.
b) Place your colleagues around you to represent your perception of working relationships – those close to you with high dependency, draw them close to you, and vice versa. Also try and represent your perception of how your colleagues work with each other in terms of dependency on each other.
c) Draw your lines to represent customer/supplier/partnership arrangements.
d) Use symbols – for example, use // to indicate barriers or difficulties, ? for areas for clarification or confusion, or any other symbols to describe the current nature of the relationship. (See T&T No 6.)

☛ List the two most important 'boundary' issues to work with, clarify or develop.

Boundary issues =
- potential areas of duplication.
- perception problems by outside world or staff in terms of who's responsible for what.
- new area for development – freedom vs no go areas.
- differences in who should take control or be responsible for certain issues, using the following symbols:

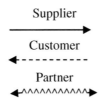

Supplier

Customer

Partner

Customer Supplier Relationships or Internal Customer Supplier Contracting – agreeing a joint improvement agenda

Fill in the form (both customer and supplier) and use it in a face to face discussion/negotiation of what to do differently.

Customer   (Name)

Developing Partnerships for excellent service
1.   The 2 main things/services/items/information I need from you in order for me to excel at my job are:-
a)
b)

2.   There are times when these have not always been delivered – and the problems this causes me are ....

3.   What , at minimum, I need..............
What at best I need...............

Can you deliver

Supplier   (Name)

1.   The reasons I/we nave not been able to deliver are.............

2.   For me/us to deliver in the future I will need from you........

Agreed actions to improve internal customer/supplier service/relationship....

DL: www.54.mwauk.com
From 54 Tools and Techniques for Business Excellence, Mike Wash (MB2000)

This exercise is most effective when there is clarity about what both parties are trying to achieve (ultimately external customer satisfaction). Also, recognising that good listening skills and a non-defensive attitude will enable good quality and honest communication. (It may be worth reviewing Contracting. See T&T No 34.)

Case study: Customer/Supplier Relationships (Internal)

A Scottish Community Health trust needed to build cooperation and teamwork across the whole organisation. Two values to be reinforced were 'one team' and 'patient focus'. Many of the support staff, such as porters, cleaners, administration staff and maintenance staff, felt like second class citizens and couldn't see how they were contributing to patient care. Workshops were run throughout the organisation deliberately mixing groups to bring together the different support staff. The first exercise was to put their names on a large sheet of paper – the patient was at the centre and they were to put their name as close to, or as far away from the patient, depending on how relevant they saw their job. Also, they had to draw lines/arrows indicating who they give and receive a service to and from. Discussions and debate related to the complexity of dependencies and a reminder of the core business – i.e. patient care took place.

The form on the previous page was then used when the group was divided into internal customer and supplier relationships. From these discussions, improvements were identified and small multi-disciplinary teams were identified to follow through the improvements identified.

T&T No:	28		
Title:	TRAINING DESIGN		
For use by:	Facilitators, Trainers, Consultants		
When to use:	Designing Training		
Also see T&T No:	31, 45, 54		
Difficulty Rating:	5	Category:	(D) Being the Best – Quality and Excellence

Training Design

The figure-of-eight diagram on page 129 shows a process that highlights some important steps and principles when designing training for organisations. Training must be based on real individual need and in the context of what the organisation needs.

The organisation 'environment' or 'climate' must be one whereby the new skills or behaviours are given every opportunity to make a difference, hence the importance that the top of this figure of eight (Learning Results) links and flows with the bottom half (Work Improvement).

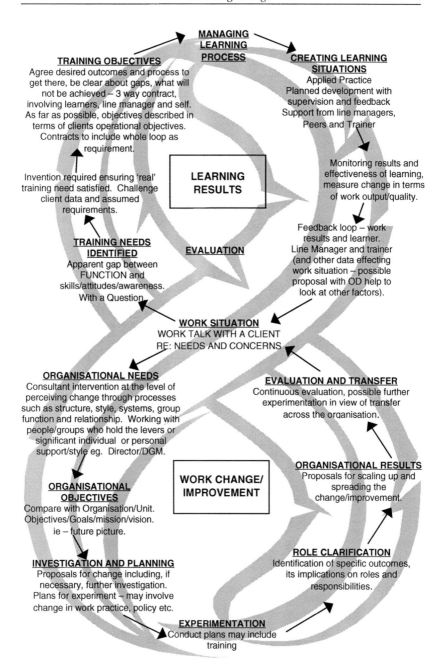

MANAGING LEARNING PROCESS

TRAINING OBJECTIVES
Agree desired outcomes and process to get there, be clear about gaps, what will not be achieved – 3 way contract, involving learners, line manager and self. As far as possible, objectives described in terms of clients operational objectives. Contracts to include whole loop as requirement.

CREATING LEARNING SITUATIONS
Applied Practice
Planned development with supervision and feedback
Support from line managers, Peers and Trainer

Invention required ensuring 'real' training need satisfied. Challenge client data and assumed requirements.

LEARNING RESULTS

Monitoring results and effectiveness of learning, measure change in terms of work output/quality.

TRAINING NEEDS IDENTIFIED
Apparent gap between FUNCTION and skills/attitudes/awareness. With a Question

EVALUATION

Feedback loop – work results and learner. Line Manager and trainer (and other data effecting work situation – possible proposal with OD help to look at other factors).

WORK SITUATION
WORK TALK WITH A CLIENT RE: NEEDS AND CONCERNS

ORGANISATIONAL NEEDS
Consultant intervention at the level of perceiving change through processes such as structure, style, systems, group function and relationship. Working with people/groups who hold the levers or significant individual or personal support/style eg. Director/DGM.

EVALUATION AND TRANSFER
Continuous evaluation, possible further experimentation in view of transfer across the organisation.

ORGANISATIONAL OBJECTIVES
Compare with Organisation/Unit. Objectives/Goals/mission/vision. ie – future picture.

WORK CHANGE/ IMPROVEMENT

ORGANISATIONAL RESULTS
Proposals for scaling up and spreading the change/improvement.

ROLE CLARIFICATION
Identification of specific outcomes, its implications on roles and responsibilities.

INVESTIGATION AND PLANNING
Proposals for change including, if necessary, further investigation. Plans for experiment – may involve change in work practice, policy etc.

EXPERIMENTATION
Conduct plans may include training

Case study

The Regional Manager (Europe) of an international airline recognised that her managers, of which there were around 60 based in 6 different countries, needed some management training. This was due to a number of requests from individuals and realising that there had been no serious investment in management development in the last eight years or so.

She asked one of her staff to come up with what was needed. This resulted in a lengthy list of training requests. My job was to identify what was really needed and deliver something appropriate, within a limited budget.

Early on, it was important to establish why the need for training now, and what was to be achieved by it? Following discussions with the European Manager, and some of her senior team, the following became the focus of a management development programme.

Context New Reality	Why Management Development Programme?	
	Behaviour/Mind Set	European MDP Outcomes
No guarantees	Self assured, self managing personal development	Confidence and framework for ongoing personal development.
Driving cost down	New ways of working, tools and techniques for process redesign and business improvement	Cause and effect analysis, Forcefield analysis, Stakeholder analysis, BPI e-learning toolkit, brainstorm and executive thinking
Production improvement	Motivational leadership, teamwork and sharing best practice	Team dynamics, chairing skills, developing leadership styles, the power of praise and the destruction of blame. Developing a learning culture.
Restriction on resources	Reduce cost of failure	Understand cost of quality concept – Pareto and act.
Increase competitiveness	Staying ahead, encouraging and rewarding innovation and service quality	Continuous improvement – the value of ongoing personal and organisation development.
Strong corporate control	Balancing local problem-solving and implementation with central expectations and demands	Strategy, communication and stakeholder analysis.
More focus on results	Clearer outcome thinking and change management ability	A framework for managing change and problem-solving.

It was agreed to run an experiment. A pilot programme for a select number of managers was run and evaluated. The feedback helped shape the programme and it was delivered to all 60 managers. Part of the design involved action learning (see T&T No 45) which encouraged learning applied to the work situation. Following the training, an evaluation process identified certain specific training needs as a follow up. A year on, and now the Regional Manager is asking how to keep the momentum of development going – so a further needs analysis has been conducted.

Real improvements were achieved both in managers' self-ability and in the way they worked together across Europe. Certain operational issues were also tackled and improved as a direct consequence of this management development programme.

Within the above process the 'figure of eight' training design principles were an important influence – i.e. starting with the work/change objectives, moving to learning results and back again to work applications.

T&T No:	29		
Title:	VALUES RATING EXERCISE FOR BUSINESS EXCELLENCE		
For use by:	Business Teams		
When to use:	Taking stock of how you are doing		
Also see T&T No:	14		
Difficulty Rating:	2	Category:	(D) Being the Best – Quality and Excellence

Values Rating Exercise for Business Excellence

The following questionnaire is best completed individually, in a team or organisation, then the results discussed openly, focusing on the item where there is a wide variation. Action plans following this discussion can result in a significant improvement agenda. (See T&T No 14.)

To what extent are we practising 'Business Excellence' Values in the way we conduct business with our customers and each other?				

Rate each statement below as follows:

0 = Not in place, or if so, not visible or generally experienced
1 = Partly in place, but we have many problems associated with this
2 = Some success, generally in place throughout the organization – still plenty of room for improvement
3 = One of our strengths – fully in place (excellence achieved)

	Rating			
Customer Focused:				
We know who our customers are	0	1	2	3
Their requirements are clear and respected	0	1	2	3
Our customers are involved in decisions concerned with how our product/service is delivered	0	1	2	3
Valuing Staff:				
We believe our people are our most important asset	0	1	2	3
We recognise the connection between success in achieving excellence and the process of empowerment	0	1	2	3
Results:				
Our successes are visible with tangible measures	0	1	2	3
We reward achievement using clear criteria	0	1	2	3
Openness:				
We review our actions regularly	0	1	2	3
We give constructive feedback to each other freely	0	1	2	3

Common Language:				
We use a common approach to Project Management	0	1	2	3
We have a common understanding of:				
a. Our vision	0	1	2	3
b. Our mission	0	1	2	3
c. Our values	0	1	2	3
d. Our priorities	0	1	2	3
Training:				
We are committed to training everyone in the organisation in the principles and essential techniques of continuous improvement.	0	1	2	3
Learning:				
We strive to be a learning organisation, in that we coach each other and review continuously to make explicit what we have learnt and the opportunities for improvement	0	1	2	3
One Direction:				
The mission, our roles and responsibilities are all aligned with and contributing to the achievement of the vision	0	1	2	3
Open Management Styles:				
Difficult issues and differences are aired and discussed with business objectives in mind	0	1	2	3
Politics are brought out of the shadows and dealt with positively	0	1	2	3
Managers are accessible and visible	0	1	2	3
Status, hierarchy and professionalism cease to be barriers	0	1	2	3
Professional Time Management:				
Time is viewed as a precious resource and hence planned consistently with priorities	0	1	2	3
There is appropriate ownership and delegation of problems	0	1	2	3
Effective Meetings:				
The most expensive management tool turned into the most efficient, by skilled preparation, facilitation and follow through	0	1	2	3
Communication:				
There are clear, open, relevant and regular briefings throughout the organisation, quality issues being the main content	0	1	2	3
Briefings are consistently conducted with active participation from the recipients – thus creating a two way briefing system	0	1	2	3
Internal customer/supplier relationships are clear and contracted service requirements are made explicit	0	1	2	3
Our external customers are regularly informed of:-				
a. Our activities	0	1	2	3
b. Our purpose	0	1	2	3
c. Our achievements	0	1	2	3
d. Our quality policies	0	1	2	3
Team Work:				
Teams are structured around customer needs and the core work purpose	0	1	2	3
There is a culture of collaborative problem-solving conducted with a high degree of team spirit	0	1	2	3

DL: www.54.mwauk.com
From 54 Tools and Techniques for Business Excellence, Mike Wash (MB2000)

T&T No:	30		
Title:	VISION SETTING		
For use by:	Organisational Leaders (e.g. CEO, Executives, Dept Heads, Team Leaders)		
When to use:	To clarify direction		
Also see T&T No:	7, 18		
Difficulty Rating:	5	Category:	(D) Being the Best – Quality and Excellence

Vision Setting

♠⃰ It is important to have a Vision because it:

- Gives direction.
- Focuses on what is important.
- Encourages team working by identifying common values thus encouraging commitment to the direction set.
- Gives an opportunity to check whether current practice is helping or hindering what is expressed in the Vision, ie are our current priorities designed in a way that will help us achieve our vision?

Vision – a definition

- An aspirational and often inspirational description of what the organisation will be like in the future, time framed: usually three to five years.
- It reflects the hopes and ambitions of its leaders following deliberation of influences, trends and values.
- It describes achievements, the working environment, perception of staff, consumers and stakeholders and can also give an indication of the organisations contribution to society.
- The measures of success will be indicated and the ideal reputation hoped for.
- Specific developments may be described, especially if they are likely to be leading edge.

Prompts for Vision building

Timescale: This depends on the speed of change within the specific market sector, but it is usually 3, 4 or 5 years.

1. What would your major achievements be
    *   in financial terms?
    *   in terms of contribution to shareholder value?
    *   in terms of projects?
2. What would your reputation be in the eyes of
    *   shareholders?
    *   customers?
    *   competitors?
3. Who would you be benchmarking against – and how would you be doing? What standard of excellence do you aspire to? What will be the critical criteria for success?
4. What size and shape will you be? (For example, what will be your number of employees, new markets, new products/services, or geographical spread?)
5. What would characterise the way you work together? What sort of working environment will it be – how will people feel working in the organisation?

The value of describing a vision can be realised when it is communicated in such a way that people can see how their individual contributions link to the overall direction.

This may involve cascading down Key Performance Indicators related to specific strategic goals. This then ensures individual goals are aligned to overall strategy.

Case study: 1: Vision Setting

As part of an organisation wide culture change programme, it was recognised that this internationally renowned Children's Hospital needed to make explicit its value based vision and communicate it in such a way that brings to life what is important in the way care is delivered.

Through a number of team meetings and workshops, the following became the basis of all decision-making and prioritisation.

C Communicating to our staff, patients, family and community with up to date relevant information.

H Honesty and openness with our ways of working, being transparent in everything we do.

I Innovation – maintaining and building on our reputation of being at the forefront of paediatric health care.

L Leadership – everyone taking responsibility for improving the way they work.

D Developing our staff to help them realise their full potential.

R Respect for children, families and each other, evident through the way we work in teams as a team.

E Energy and enthusiasm creating a healing, creative and healthy work environment.

N National pride, demonstrated by our contribution to research and recognition for best practice.

Case study: 2: Vision Statement

An engineering director from an airline company wrote this vision statement following a workshop where the vision prompts were used to help make explicit the kind of department he wanted.

'Our team is the key to success. A multicultural workforce that is well integrated at all levels is a priority. The management style shall be the motivating force, leading from the front and by example, embracing change. The work ethic shall be one of openness and honesty with a clear belief we can make a success of the future. Creativity and innovation will be rewarded as will responsibility and calculated risk taking in pursuit of the goal'.

We will achieve best levels of **safety**, **reliability** and **cost** for our Airline and our customers.

Our **TEAM** is the key to success: highly skilled technically and commercially, working **openly**, **honestly** and **creatively**, **embracing change** and managing globally.

T&T No:	31		
Title:	WORKSHOP DESIGN AND FACILITATION		
For use by:	Trainers, Facilitators, Managers as Change Agents		
When to use:	Designing Events		
Also see T&T No:	28, 51		
Difficulty Rating:	5	Category:	(D) Being the Best – Quality and Excellence

Workshop Design and Facilitation

A learning organisation must take every opportunity to learn and re-learn the lessons that will add value at every level.

Sometimes learning opportunities arise spontaneously, and sometimes the opportunities must be created and facilitated.

The guidelines offered here are aimed at helping managers develop their current personal and organisational skills towards a facilitative style that will be empowering for the people within the organisation that encounter it. It does not stand in isolation, but can be utilised alongside coaching and problem-solving skills, and may be thought of as an extension of the role of the manager as a change agent or facilitator.

What follows is a brief description of skills and how they are used in training, a training design package which asks you the questions you will need to get the design together, a sample session plan sheet and an awareness exercise regarding a workshop environment.

Training design bullet points

Objectives:
- Each session should have clear behavioural objectives.
- Objectives should be strategy-driven.
- Objectives are best shared and/or agreed with the group, promoting ownership.

Vision/ Mission:	• Training courses ought to have their own vision and mission. It will feed objectives.
	• What are your ultimate outcomes?
	• How do they relate to organisational strategy?

| Planning: | • Step – by – step planning is essential to successful outcomes in training. |
| | • Use the planning guide to get your bigger ideas. into manageable sessions. Good sequence promotes interest. |

Attention Span:	• Most people have an attention span of 20 minutes or less.
	• Attention is attenuated by things like fatigue, a full stomach or monotony.
	• Break up your timing and activities to combat this.
	• Variety is the spice of learning.

| Presentation Style: | • Use different styles to back up different points. |
| | • Identify which styles you can use to raise energy, consolidate learning points, motivate the group and direct energy. |

Timing:	• A key feature in training.
	• A course works best if it is 'timely', as do interventions.
	• A well timed course stimulates interest and adds discipline to the group.

Self Presentation:	• The best way to learn is to teach.
	• Make sure you identify your areas of strength and development.
	• Structure yourself and prepare accordingly.

Rehearsal:	• Run through your whole presentation a few times.
	• Use key points on file cards as prompts.
	• Test the session out on an honest friend who understands how to give feedback!

Reflection:
- Build in time for reflection/consolidation.
- Help participants answer their own questions at the end of the session.
- Remember – incubation of new information may lead to the development of new ideas.

Session planning

①	②	③

• Who are all my customers?
  o Internal
  o External
 	
• What do I think they need from training?
 	
• What do they think they need?
 	
• What is a realistic assessment of their level of ability?
 	
• What knowledge base do I need to deliver effectively?
 	
• What part/aspect of the presentation will provide leverage (Pareto)
  o The key points
  o i.e. how does the session:
    a) relate to strategy
    b) add value to the organisation
	• What's the best possible range of outcomes?
	
	• What are all the outcomes I want to see in place?
	
	• What's the least compromise I can accept?
	
	• What do I want the wider effects of the session to be? (morale etc)
	
	• What are my personal goals?
	
	• What are my aims for the group?
	
	• What are my objectives for the group?
	
	• Do the aims/ objectives match the identified needs?
	
	• Are there likely to be any unintended effects from the session, and do they need to be factored in to my planning?
		• What are all the things that will help me deliver:
		  o Methods
		  o Sequence
		  o Venue
		  o Facilities
		  o Visual aids
		  o Marketing
		  o Administration
		  o Possible hindrances
		  o Possible helps
		  o Timing
		    ▪ of session itself
		    ▪ of session in relation to other aspects of development
		
		• Step by step plan

Case study

The following workshop design uses a 'template' similar to that offered in Meeting Management (see T&T No 51). Its content is created as a result of answering the questions offered in the 'session planning' above. This template design then becomes the manager's/trainer's guide to move the group forward in a timely and developmental way.

Outline design of MDP – Workshop 1

Group 1: 5/6 March   Group 2: 7/8 June   Group 3: 28/29 August
Venue: TBC (Bangkok)

Time	Item	Who	Purpose	Process	Materials/Notes etc
Day One					
0845	Welcome	MW	To see who's who and gain insight into each other's work challenges and culture.	Split into countries/ports. Prepare flipchart presentation – e.g. **BKK** (Hopes and expectations / Current work challenges / Our Culture)	Flipchart/Pens Blue Tac
0930	The Programme and Business Context	GH	To clarify detail and use of workbook. To understand 'Why AMDP?'. Highlight and agree groundrules.	Input on programme, learning styles, importance of reflection. Give out handout reflecting RGM's script and AMDP outcomes. read and discuss in small groups – highlight issues and questions.	? Park list flipchart Pens/Handouts/ Paper
1000	A Model for Change	GH	To give an overview of Model B.	Presentation.	Projector, white board
1015	BREAK				
1030	Foundation Skills	MW	To revise, develop interpersonal skills related to effective listening and understanding.	NVC exercise. Model active listening & empathy. 3 groups – shape up skills.	2 rooms Cards with skills on

Time	Item	Who	Purpose	Process	Materials/Notes etc
1130	Stage 1	GH	To apply skills to work related issues regards 'current situation' – i.e. what's really going on?	Input, model, illustrate, triad work with feedback process.	Criteria for selecting working partners. Rehearse role play.
1200	Practice	GH MW JL	To practise the skills.	Work in 3's.	Trainers allocate to particular triad.
1245	Review	JL	To highlight learning (and introduce concept of learning partners – to choose over lunch).	Open questions.	Criteria for Learning Partners.
1300	LUNCH				
1400	Stage 2	MW GH	To practise vision prompts, goal setting and commitment testing.	Input, model, practise in 3's.	Rehearse, organise.
1515	BREAK				
1530	Stage 3	MW GH	To practise brainstorm strategies for action, best fit and force field analysis.	Input, model, practise in 3's.	Ensure use of flipcharts.
1630	Harrison Assessments	GH	To understand the basic theory.	Presentation.	Reports available.
1700	Making sense of the results	GH MW JL	To understand one's own profile.	Pairs work, applying foundation skills to help each other gain insights. MW/GH/JL in support.	Summary reports for trainers.
1800	Learning Partners	JL	To 'buddy' up to help challenge/support each other throughout the programme.	Work with learning partner in structured format.	Space available. Contract meeting up later.
1830	BREAK				
1930	Drinks				
2000	Dinner				

T&T No:	32		
Title:	CHECKLISTS		
For use by:	Those involved in Action Planning or Quality Control		
When to use:	Before a project/process or after a procedure		
Also see T&T No:	40, 51		
Difficulty Rating:	2	Category:	(E) Work Smarter

Checklists

What is it?

A checklist is a list of things to be done or items to be obtained. It is a simple way of remembering what to do and then checking that you have done it.

When to use it?

Checklists can be used at any point in the project management process and are particularly useful for:
- Preparing lists of material/equipment/activities required.
- Collecting data.
- Preparing standard practices and procedures.
- Constructing action plans.

What does it achieve?

Rather than having to rely on your memory or the memory of others, a checklist provides a useful way of deciding – and remembering – the What, Where, Who, When and the How of doing things. It enables standardisation and can be an important part of a quality process.

Examples might be:
- Helping you to make sure you perform all of your tasks in order to ensure completion and standardisation.

- Making sure you know what you have done so you don't backtrack, or repeat unnecessarily – i.e. over checking.

Key steps

- Brainstorm (see T&T No 40) any items or steps/actions associated with the task or procedure.
- Record on list – place them in a sequence or group that aids efficiency.
- Record who, what, where and when for each item on list.
- (For each item – if it's a large project or procedure and ensure the owner or leader for each item is identified.)
- Copy checklist to all involved.
- Tick items as they are done.
- ✔ Set up a review meeting if more than one person involved to identify progress and to learn from blocks to success. (See T&T No 51.)

The following is a checklist we use in preparation for delivering a training workshop:-

Checklist for things to take/have available:-

Workshop 1	ALS 1	Workshop 2	ALS 2
Files and Workbook 1 (1 per participant)	Handout – A process for Action Learning Sets (ALS)	Workbook 2 (for them to insert in file)	Personal letters (done at Workshop 1)
Flipchart (supplied by hotel)	Handout – Action Learning sets (ALS) involve	Best in Class CD (Copies)	Certificates (signed and dated)
Flipchart pens	Handout – ALS1 Notes	Blindfolds	
Blue Tac	Handout – ALS 2 Notes	Blue Tac	
Pink Cards with Quotes	Handout – The Johari Window	Flipchart pens (flipchart – hotel)	
Name game white card (small)	Handout – Action Learning – the skills to practise	Games (Train/Pyramid/T's)	
Pink question cards (1 – 12)		Rope (big & shrinking exercise)	

Workshop 1	ALS 1	Workshop 2	ALS 2
Handout: Group application & facilitation		Leadership Quotes	
Handout: Ladder of Inference		Envelopes for '2 dog cards'	
Camera (for group photo)		Dog Metaphor Cards	
Envelopes (for letters to self)		Dog Feedback Cards	
54 Approaches to Brickwall Management book		Acetates with Dogs	
		Time line Ribbon	
		Scissors	
		Handout: Challenging Skills	
		Handout: Psychological Time	
		Flipchart sheet with groundrules from Workshop 1 written up.	
		Handout: Email Management	
		Post it notes	

T&T No:	33		
Title:	CONTINGENCY PLANNING (Risk Management)		
For use by:	All those involved in implementing change		
When to use:	Prior to implementation		
Also see T&T No:	17		
Difficulty Rating:	3	Category:	(E) Work Smarter

Contingency Planning

Or – what to do *if* things go wrong!
Or – what to do *when* things go wrong!
All managers should know that it is not 'if' but 'when' because things inevitably will go wrong – hence the importance of contingency planning.

What is it?

A contingency plan is an outline of the what, who, when, and how. All of which need to be addressed to ensure that any potential barriers to the implementation of a project are handled in a pro-active manner. This can involve a detailed risk assessment and for each risk – an action plan to prevent and or deal with each eventuality.

When to use it

The preparation of a contingency plan should be undertaken prior to the implementation of an action plan or project. It can aid in the run up to action, in that it should identify helping and hindering factors (see T&T No 17).

What does it achieve?

Preparation of a contingency plan permits you to identify 'what could go

145

wrong' and for you to list the necessary steps you may need to take to ensure that the implementation of your action plan or project goes as smoothly as possible – i.e. identifying the risks and the process by which you can minimise each one.

Key steps

- ✓ Define desired outcome.
- Identify all possible impediments to achieving this outcome.
- Consider probability of impediments occurring.
- Produce preventative action plans.

Typical contingency plan summary

(can be used as part of a Risk Assurance framework)

Potential Problem	Who	What	Where	When	Likelihood of RISK occurring * (1 – 3)	Potential Impact * (1 – 3)	Action Plan Ref.
	Lead person responsible.	Description of action	Location or department.	Timescale for preventative action and date for review.			

*Risk: 1 = unlikely, 2 = possible, 3 = likely
Impact: 1 = minimal, 2 = serious, 3 = devastating

High and low risk can be determined by multiplying likelihood and impact.

Case study: Contingency Planning and

Scenario Testing

Every year, the NHS in the UK builds robust contingency plans and risk management plans. Contingency plans are designed in detail for potential crises, emergencies, epidemics, flu crises, winter pressures on beds and more.

This involves clear lines of accountability and communication plans in the event of an occurrence.

Many organisations rehearse, or role play, the event to learn and help prepare should it ever become reality.

Airlines are required to have an emergency response plan in the event of major delays and accidents. They train all their front line staff in the skills and behaviours needed to cope with such an event. www.emergplansoc.org.uk gives a comprehensive description of the resources, preparation and planning needed in these types of situations.

Scenario testing is a tool to help focus on the key areas of crisis probability relevant to the nature of the business – oil spillage, flu epidemic, national grid failure, IT system failure etc.

This can take weeks, if not months, so it's important to identify the probability of scenarios using a Risk Assurance framework that scores possible scenarios in a matrix of Probability Hi/Lo & Impact Hi/Lo. This will give an indication as to where to focus further detailed planning and data gathering.

Scenario testing requires you to put the scenario at the centre and work outwards with teams looking at the likely events, externally and internally, as a consequence.

This flags up what data is missing and, therefore, required to establish robust contingency plans. For example, in a Flu epidemic the scenario might be as follows: hospitals are expecting to lose 30% of their workforce within 5 days not because of flu but because of Carer responsibilities at home – it is possible schools will close within 3 days! This is a high probability/high impact area for scenario testing and contingency planning.

Contingency plans need 'table top' testing every six to twelve months because things, systems and knowledge changes. Full rehearsal exercises are often prohibitive in costs, but should be budgeted for and scheduled at least every 2 years – dependent upon the scale of the disaster.

T&T No:	34		
Title:	CONTRACTING		
For use by:	Anyone		
When to use:	At the beginning of 1:1 or team meetings		
Also see T&T No:	2, 12, 39		
Difficulty Rating:	2	Category:	(E) Work Smarter

Contracting

Agreeing a contract

Activities and behaviours in the early stages of a relationship, whether with your staff, a colleague, your boss or a client, are crucial in setting future direction and tone. This needs careful planning in the light of the interpretation of the relevant 'agenda'. You need to establish to your own satisfaction the answers to five related questions:

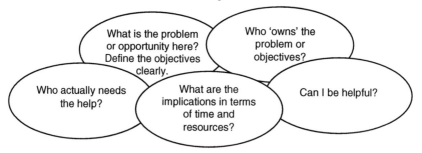

In clarifying these basic questions, some major issues must be confronted and managed within the developing relationship. Listening carefully is crucial at this stage, especially in terms of:

Content: What are the facts you are hearing? What information? What are the person's expectations? What is the intended outcome?

Process: What issues come across about control, authority and trust? What methods and/or approach is intended or proposed?

Feelings: What clues to these are you picking up? What's the level of motivation, commitment, risk and anxiety?

Elements of a good contract

1. Mutual understanding of need for two or more parties to work together.
2. Recognition that each party needs something from the other.
3. A clear exchange of wants and expectations from each other.
4. A process to clarify understanding and agreement on both sides

    Usually involves:
    - Clarification of purpose and/or intended outcome.
    - Time involved.
    - Other resource implications.

5. ☛ Commitment to work together to achieve agreed goal (at 3 levels).

    - Cognitive   - I agree with the idea/task
    - Behavioural   - I will act on this and do certain things
    - Emotional   - I feel it's importance and sense of priority and want to do this.

6. A Review Process

    Usually involves:
    - Indication of measure for success
    - A process to review progress and learning.

The above refers to a personal contract between individuals or groups. The same principles apply when formally contracting services. However, in a 'supplier' contract, detail concerning the nature of services and how they will be delivered needs to be explicit. Clauses would include issues related to time of delivery, cancellation, penalty clauses for late delivery, quality standards, guarantees etc.

149

Case study: Contracting

(in context of managing your time and the demands made upon you)
(See T&T No 39.)

A few simple questions will significantly improve efficiency of dialogue ensuring clearer expectations from both partners – i.e. a contract.

Staff: Can I see you for a minute?

Boss: Do you mean a minute? How long and why?

Staff: Well, maybe 20 minutes to discuss some difficulties I'm having with this project.

Boss: OK, but what exactly are you wanting?

Staff: Some feedback about whether the next steps I am about to take are suitable and if I'm being realistic or not.

Boss: OK. When do you want to meet?

Staff: This afternoon?

Boss: Make it 2pm.

Staff: OK – see you then!

Contract made!!!

T&T No:	35		
Title:	DECISION ANALYSIS		
For use by:	Anyone or key team meetings on direction		
When to use:	When clarity is important regards choice		
Also see T&T No:	15, 16		
Difficulty Rating:	3	Category:	(E) Work Smarter

Decision Analysis

What is it?

Decision analysis is a technique to assist you, or a group, to determine the choice of an action to take, taking account of the objectives, what alternatives there are and what risks are involved.

When to use it

- Deciding which solution to implement.
- Deciding which course of action to take.

What does it achieve?

When a decision is required, and people are given the opportunity to contribute towards the choices being considered, they will be more inclined to work as a team and have commitment to the decision made. The team members will be able to share information, and discuss their relevant positions and priorities, so that the reason for any decision is more readily accepted and understood. The more explicit the criteria used for decision-making, the more chance of it being followed through with agreement and ownership.

As the differing opinions within the team have been aired, the process of making the decision is less biased and the decision itself is more balanced.

When faced with a number of options, decision analysis provides a structured route towards the best all-round decision. These options should be considered by assessing:-

- The potential drawbacks of each option.
- All aspects to be considered against each option.
- All aspects to be considered for each option.
- Whether they will achieve the objective.

Key steps

- Define decision required.
- Decide decision criteria – 'Musts' and 'Wants'
- Select options.
- Rate options.
- Look for adverse consequences and unforeseen benefits.
- Analyse and evaluate.

⬜ Diagrams and 'decision-making trees' can be useful visual aids to track the discussion and record the issues.

Here is an example of a decision tree that illustrates basic steps:

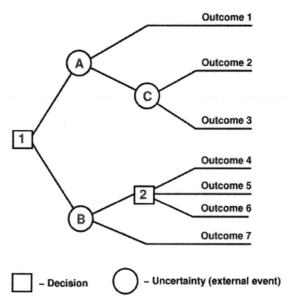

Case study: Decision Analysis

I recall helping a national utility company in the UK decide how to manage a massive 'downsize' or redundancy situation.

When to announce, should it be phased, how to prepare the managers, what support should be available for those affected, how do we manage those left etc?

We certainly used a version of the method described here (make explicit the options, identify the pros and cons for each, and follow through making explicit the criteria used for a particular decision).

We also used cost benefit analysis (see T&T No 15). The effect and value of spending time making explicit how decisions were made in this situation paid off in that the quality of communication about the whole programme was much better.

The organisations value of open, honest and transparent communication was in evidence through the regular bulletins, briefings and eventually the 'counselling skills workshop for managers' because of the emphasis put on decision analysis in the early planning phase of the redundancy programme.

T&T No:	36		
Title:	DELEGATION		
For use by:	Supervisors		
When to use:	When workload needs managing		
Also see T&T No:	12, 39, 45		
Difficulty Rating:	4	Category:	(E) Work Smarter

Delegation

Why should I delegate?

Managers or supervisors should delegate any task which somebody else can do.....

1. ....better than they can. Managers should ensure that they are taking advantage of anybody who has work-related, specialist knowledge, so that the talents of individuals work for everyone's benefit.
2. ....cheaper than they can, because certain staff get paid less than you.
3. ....with better timing – 'the less than ideal solution at the right time is better than the otherwise ideal solution at the wrong time'.
4. ....as a contribution to staff training and development. If you, as a manager, feel that you cannot trust a subordinate with jobs which you know you should not be tackling, then you have a training job on your hands – and training includes delegation.

What should I not delegate?

As a manager or supervisor, you should not delegate any high-level tasks which require your full attention. Such tasks include:

1. Overall policy for your operation,
2. Overall planning.
3. Personnel matters – selection, training, development and appraisal of your immediate subordinates.
4. Promotion, praise and disciplinary action for your immediate subordinates.
5. Accountability.

How to delegate

- Ensure that your staff understands the complete task to be achieved. Why they are doing it. What is the target? When must it be completed and to what standard?
- ☛ Give them the necessary authority – define the limits and make sure that they understand them. The delegation cannot work successfully if the person has to come back repeatedly asking for permission to proceed.
- Inform any others who might be affected by your decision. A failure to do so will create unnecessary antagonism, conflict and tension.
- ◀ Remember that you cannot delegate a task, which is new to someone, without giving training or supportive coaching. Your member of staff may not have carried out the delegated task before.
- Prepare a training/coaching plan (see T&T No 45), and remember it may take some time before they can carry out the task as well as you can. Eventually they will, so be patient.
- ☛ Allow the individual to reverse a decision themselves. Never countermand their decisions publicly.
- When the member of staff takes over the task, they accept responsibility for their actions; you, however, must accept the accountability for any decisions you delegate.

Following up

- Create the opportunity to take feedback on progress, but not too much as this may convey low confidence or mistrust. Review progress regularly; delegation without control is abdication.
- Give the individual as much freedom as possible to use his/her skills; don't always provide answers but give some help as to where the answer may be found.
- Don't be hasty in criticising shortfalls. Maybe you wouldn't have done it that way, but it's the outcome of the delegated task that is important.
- ☛ Regular appraisal of your staff must take place, with feedback as soon as possible, giving private and public praise for any task completed well.

Successful delegation lies within the key questions:

💣

- 'What should I be doing and what should I not be doing?'
- 'How can I best equip each member of staff to do what they should be doing?'

Do:	Don't:
Take time to plan the delegation properly	Specify how the job has to be done
Be prepared to let go and allow proper delegation	Take all the credit
Be specific about expected outcomes	Always delegate to the same person
Negotiate the delegated activity with the person/s concerned	Leave the person without any support

Case study: Delegation Skills

Oliver was a recently promoted operational manager of a cake manufacturer. His boss asked me to see if I could offer him support as he was aware that his current working regime was unsustainable – 12 hours a day, 6 days a week and Sunday evening catching up with emails.

Oliver had worked for the firm most of his life and was an expert on all things related to production.

On his desk, his laptop was continuously wired into hour-by-hour fluctuations in sales, orders, production lines and breakdowns. As soon as there was any variation he would be on the phone to find out why. Staff were continuously coming to him for help and advice. I sat in on one of his daily operational review meetings. Afterwards, I asked him if all his meetings were like that – i.e. 80% of the time, Oliver was talking and solving problems.

When the overall picture of how he worked was put to him, combined with an acknowledgement that he was getting stressed and his home life was beginning to be affected, he realised his current way of working was unsustainable.

We explored alternatives, and the focus of his development was in terms of how he could delegate more. He needed to move from being an expert problem solver and advice giver to a 'manager'. This involved trusting more, letting go of the daily need for monitoring, asking more open questions to facilitate his team to manage, rather than them being dependent on Oliver for most decisions and problem-solving.

With some experimentation and coaching, Oliver started to work smarter.

T&T No:	37		
Title:	EMAIL MANAGEMENT		
For use by:	All		
When to use:	If you are spending more than 10% of your time on email		
Also see T&T No:	13, 39		
Difficulty Rating:	1	Category:	(E) Work Smarter

Email Management

One of the most common causes of frustration, in terms of taking up management time, is the time it takes to read and 'deal' with emails.

The exacerbation of emails is the result of the following:

- Easy, quick, convenient.
- The sender is in control of the message – i.e. it is sent out on own terms.
- Used as a way of 'covering ones back' – i.e. copying people in for information and claim you have communicated.
- Reduces the risk of rejection.
- Satisfy one's conscience in terms of 'completed a task'.
- Perceived as saving time.
- Used to avoid difficult relationships and/or issues.

I would like you to consider this statement:

Sending an email is a very poor form of communication
(this is particularly so for internal email)

💣 Communication is a two way process where the sender gets feedback as to how the message has been received.

Email is the poorest form of communication used within companies.

On average a typical manager may spend between one and two hours dealing with emails of which 20% may be important/meaningful. This is an incredible waste of resource. Some managers can spend 50% of their time responding to and sending out emails.

Sending a 'message received' or even a written response is only a small proportion of how the message was received and understood compared with a telephone conversation or, even better, a face to face meeting.

People in organisations are getting 'socially lazy' – i.e. they would rather send an email than walk down the corridor for a face to face interaction.

In organisations where there is an element of fear – emails are sent 'just in case'. So managers are copied in 'just in case' they need or want to know!

♦ For an efficient email culture – follow these guidelines:

1. Do not use emails to chat, catch up or gossip – use the phone or face to face.
2. Do not copy 'just in case'. Only copy people in if they have asked to be kept informed.
3. Do not print out emails and file – this is duplication – have an efficient email file system.
4. When sending emails be clear as to its purpose in the 'subject' heading, stating:
   • for information only (urgent, important, interesting)
   • for action by you by date
   • for decision by you by date
   • for feedback regards _____ by _____.
5. The clearer you are as to why you have sent the email the easier the receiver will be able to judge how to respond.
6. Do not use block capitals as it can indicate SHOUTING and be misinterpreted as abusive.
7. When reading emails, ignore those that don't have a clear purpose.
8. Deal with those that require action.
9. When replying – ask yourself – would a phone call or quick face to face be better.
10. You should rarely email anyone who works in the same office area as yourself.

Organisations or departments which have a clear policy on to how to manage emails have a chance to avoid being subsumed.

Some are considering having an internal email-free day to get over the message that it's better to talk.

Ensure you have an effective spam filter and also communicate your email policy to your customers and suppliers – it's amazing how it will improve relationships.

When responding to unclear emails, use the phrases:

- See me!
- Talk to me!
- Yes.
- No.
- Don't understand.

People will eventually get the message that emails are the least effective form of communication.

T&T No:	38		
Title:	PRESENTATION SKILLS		
For use by:	All		
When to use:	Need to communicate to a group or several groups a consistent clear message		
Also see T&T No:	51		
Difficulty Rating:	4	Category:	(E) Work Smarter

Presentation Skills

To stand up in front of an audience and convey information in a way that is meaningful, relevant and interesting requires a set of skills that are often assumed to be a natural part of any manager's make-up. This is not the case. The majority of people, even the most senior of managers, are nervous at the prospect of delivering presentations, particularly if there is much depending on the outcome.

From the following preparation checklist it can be seen that for a professional and effective presentation, a detailed analysis needs to take place concerning what you want to communicate, why and to whom, and the best method to get the key points over. As a rough guideline, it is estimated that a one-hour presentation should take three hours' preparation. This does not include time to rehearse in front of a friendly but constructive audience. So, for those who think it is just a matter of talking through some prepared slides, this section may come as a bit of a surprise.

The following checklist should help in the preparation:

1. Planning 💣※

a)   The outcome I want from this session is:-
     (What specific reaction and actions do you want from your audience?)

b)   My objectives are the following. Influence of:
     i)   Knowledge
          (What facts or new information do you want to help your audience to understand?)

ii)   Attitudes
(You want them to see things from a different perspective; convince, influence or sell)
iii) Beliefs
(Why is it important, what connections to organisation and/or personal enhancement can be made? Are links to values and strategy clear?)
iv) Decisions
(Be clear about options, choices and consequences of each)

2. Development

a)   What resources and sources of information do I need for this presentation?
b)   Content
  i)   What must I get across in the allotted time?
  ii)   What could I get across in the allotted time?
  iii) What should I get across in the allotted time?
c)   Timing
  Many people either over-estimate or under-estimate how long a presentation takes. A rough guide could be two minutes per slide.
d)   Overall organisation. Every presentation should have a beginning, middle and an end. A useful guide could be:
  i.   Tell 'em what you're going to tell 'em. (Introduction)
  ii.   Tell 'em.   (Main body)
  iii. Tell 'em what you have told 'em.   (Summary of key parts)
e)   Reference notes (file cards are useful)
  i)   My reference card bullet points are:
  ii)   My OHP/flipchart or presentation slide prompts are:
  iii) Are my cards numbered in sequence: yes/no
  iv)   My opening sentence is:
  v)   My closing sentence is:

3. Preparation

a)   Rehearsal
  i)   My rehearsal partner/audience is:
  ii)   The time we have set aside for rehearsal is:
      Day: Date:
      From: To:

Do's and don'ts of presentations

DO ☛	DON'T ☚
Make your presentation slides or flipcharts clear – do not put too much information on one slide/sheet.	Present small, complex and confusing script on slides or flipcharts.
Check all your equipment beforehand.	Assume everything will work.
Sit where the audience will sit to test out what they will see.	Position people behind pillars or with their backs to the screen.
Prepare your material well in advance.	Leave the copying or alterations to the last minute.
Check with your client/ audience their expectations; know who is attending.	Present something that is inappropriate to the agenda or what is expected.
Introduce clearly yourself and what you are about to present to them, the outcomes you hope to achieve and the role you want them to play – eg. questions afterwards or participatory.	Apologise for the presentation, or show any lack of conviction.
Speak clearly, vary your pitch and tone and engage in eye contact with your audience.	Mumble or speak to the screen.
Use a pointer or pen on the overhead projector or screen.	Assume your audience knows the fact that you are referring to on the slide or chart.
Stand aside of the screen.	Block the view of the client/audience by standing between them and the screen.
Move appropriately; remove any distractions (e.g. a pocketful of coins).	Stand rigid or jump about; jingle keys or coins in your pocket.
When asked a question that you are not sure of, check that you have understood what the question is.	Be defensive and engage in argument.
Speak with belief and enthusiasm – remind yourself of the importance of what you are doing.	Be trapped by your own nervousness and self-consciousness.
Ensure that appropriate handouts are available during or after the presentation.	Let people take copious notes only to tell them afterwards that handouts are available.
Use bullet points.	Read script from the screen.
Give time for the audience to read the screen/chart.	Talk over your audience while they are reading something else.
Use appropriate humour.	Tell jokes that are irrelevant to the presentation.
Keep an eye on timing and control the pace.	Get sidetracked – you are in charge.
Summarise appropriately, and thank your audience.	End abruptly without clarifying what the presentation was all about.

DL: www.54.mwauk.com
From 54 Tools and Techniques for Business Excellence, Mike Wash (MB2000)

By using the 'Do' part of the presentation preparation as a checklist, you can review your own effectiveness before and after each session. This can be enhanced by using a self critique sheet and making a personal assessment. To validate your perceptions of what actually happened, ask for feedback from a member of the audience at an appropriate time afterwards.

You could use a self-critique check list to compare how you think you did, with the experience of an audience member. You can design your own self-critique checklist around particular points of feedback or development you are interested in. an example is set out below.

Self-critique for presentations

	Expect to:	Did:
Use appropriate spoken English.		
Speak clearly and unhurriedly.		
Vary pace and pitch, use visual aids, allow time for thought or questions.		
Maintain eye contact, even when feeling under pressure.		
Involve audience appropriately.		
Appear enthusiastic.		
Which Mannerisms show?		
Pet phrases.		
Avoid jargon.		
Avoid talking `down' to the audience.		
Timing.		
Response to Questions.		

DL: www.54.mwauk.com
From 54 Tools and Techniques for Business Excellence, Mike Wash (MB2000)

T&T No:	39		
Title:	TIME MANAGEMENT		
For use by:	All		
When to use:	Personal efficiency, prioritisation		
Also see T&T No:	13, 37		
Difficulty Rating:	3	Category:	(E) Work Smarter

Time Management

There is no such thing as 'not enough time' – there's always enough time – it's how you use it, and how you prioritise, that will determine the degree of so called time-pressure.

There is a direct connection between stress and 'burn-out' at work, and the inability to assert your own needs in managing your own time and priorities.

Some general principles for time management

1. Be clear about your priorities in life (what is it you want?).
2. Have clarity about your role and responsibilities and how they fit together with business priorities.
3. Be open about your discipline and efforts at time management:
    –   engage the support of your team and fellow managers.
4. Plan specific time slots for meetings (start and finish times).
    –   prepare well for each meeting.
5. Minimise interruptions:
    –   filter and offer a planned meeting time if more appropriate.
    –   plan specific time for open door policy.
    –   sort out priorities.
    –   plan time for less important ones.
6. Filter and categorise paperwork:
    –   plan specific times for dealing with it.
    –   mark with a cross when seen – don't come back to it!

7. Ask yourselves these questions three times a day:-
    –   Should I be doing this?
    –   Is this the most efficient way of doing this?
    –   Am I making the most of my time right now?

The following concepts of psychological time and 'now' time can help put things in perspective, reduce stress and remind us of what is really important.

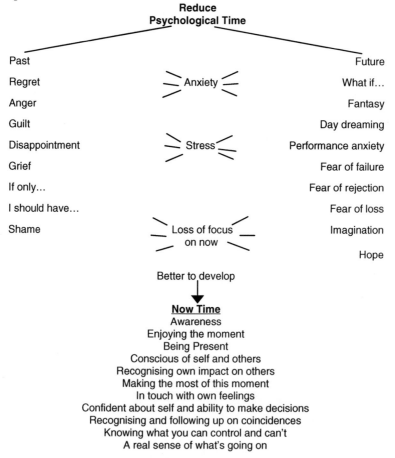

Reduce Psychological Time

Past	Future
Regret	Anxiety	What if...
Anger		Fantasy
Guilt		Day dreaming
Disappointment	Stress	Performance anxiety
Grief		Fear of failure
If only...		Fear of rejection
I should have...		Fear of loss
Shame	Loss of focus on now	Imagination
		Hope

Better to develop

Now Time
Awareness
Enjoying the moment
Being Present
Conscious of self and others
Recognising own impact on others
Making the most of this moment
In touch with own feelings
Confident about self and ability to make decisions
Recognising and following up on coincidences
Knowing what you can control and can't
A real sense of what's going on

For further hints and tips for Time Management, refer to *54 Approaches to Brickwall Management, Managing Change at Work*, Mike Wash, published MB2000, 2006, and to *www.mwauk.com*.

166

T&T No:	40		
Title:	BRAINSTORMING		
For use by:	Any Team Leader		
When to use:	Encourage creativity and/or problem analysis/solution finder		
Also see T&T No:	13, 22		
Difficulty Rating:	1	Category:	(F) Creative Techniques

Brainstorming

What is it?

Brainstorming is a technique which encourages creative thinking and the generation of ideas.

It is simple to operate (if the rules of brainstorming are clearly explained and agreed beforehand) and can often add life to a group that is stuck and frustrated with a problem.

When to use it

- Generating a list of problems and opportunities.
- Identifying possible data requirements.
- Developing ideas for solutions.
- Generating possible solutions.
- Developing action plans.

What does it achieve?

Providing the rules and principles are followed, brainstorming can achieve the following results:-

- Many ideas are produced in a short time.
- Enable participants to both contribute individually and to benefit from ideas generated by others.
- Encourage the generation of 'unusual', 'wild' or creative ideas.

167

- Encourage deeper thinking about particular problems.
- Create the environment which will enhance group activity of teamwork.
- Provide a more positive environment in which to approach problem-solving.

Key steps

1. Set the ground rules – check everyone understands (see rules for Brainstorming).
2. Agree time limit.
3. Assign one or two scribes.
4. Record all ideas.
5. Prioritise ideas through voting – Pareto. (See T&T No 13.)
6. Incubate/reflect – take a break and come back to it later.
7. Review list and discuss in more detail.
8. Agree the final list and choose which ones to act upon.

♠☀ Rules for brainstorming

1. *Don't analyse, be specific.*
   Brainstorming is about getting as many ideas to work with as possible, with an economy on time. Encourage all group members to contribute, no matter how trivial or 'off the wall' the suggestion is. Short, succinct statements are better than elaborate description. Be as specific as you can.

2. *Help everyone contribute.*
   ⋔ As a group, try and include suggestions from as many members as possible. Keep an eye out for quiet members who may be hesitant in offering ideas. Help those with lots of ideas to give others a chance.

   Use different methods of participation – for example, 'one last chance' then go round everyone. Offer the pen to everyone and start writing up themselves (perhaps in smaller groups).

3. *No criticism.*
   Help group members to avoid the trap of evaluating each others ideas at this stage. Just now, all ideas are equal. Point out that this applies

to the way we think, too. If anyone has an idea, then thinks it is not worth offering, encourage them to offer it anyway – it might help. Criticism is a real barrier to creativity. If necessary, remind the group of the rule that evaluation must wait.

4. *Freewheel and encourage creative wild ideas too!*
    Encourage random suggestions, even if they aren't immediately practicable. If one idea sparks off others, record these too, even if they are similar. From what may be seen as a wild idea – a spark of creative possibility may develop.

5. *Go for quantity, not quality.*
    Encourage the group to list as many ideas as possible, no matter how small or large they seem. Give a group a goal (e.g. a group of 12 people in 15 minutes should be able to generate over 100 items!).

6. *Record all ideas.*
    ☐ Make sure everyone's contributions are noted. Fix full flipchart sheets in view so that they can spark other ideas. Use a flipchart, large pens; clear writing – so everyone can see ideas as they are written down. If the ideas come thick and fast, enlist someone to help record them. Two people recording need to work closely together taking alternative ideas – ask the group for co-operation – timing and flow is important here.

7. *Incubate.*
    Allow time for reflection (incubation) on listed ideas. If new ideas occur to people during reflection time, encourage them to record them, add them to the list. Incubation should occur prior to evaluation of the ideas listed.

What do I need?

To run an effective brainstorming session, the following things will help:
*   ☐ A quiet area/room for the group to work in.
*   A flipchart and marker pens.
*   Blue-tac.
*   Wall space to place flipcharts.

What to do with the outcome (List)

Options:

a) Group them – discuss and recognise links, themes – break them down into groupings that have related issues/ideas.
b) Pareto using individual votes. (See T&T No 13.)
c) Choose those that need developing further – assign them or ask for volunteers to work the ideas up in more detail.
d) Post the output to a wider audience and ask for further ideas.
e) Identify a sub-group to evaluate the ideas and present back a short list of those worth actioning.

Hints and tips – brainstorming prompts

When a group begins to dry up with ideas – use open prompts – such as:

- Anything else?
- What systems?
- What people?
- What things?
- What places?
- Who has been successful in this?
- Potential helpers, models etc
- What's the craziest idea you can think of? (Out of the craziest ideas can come a new realistic one that can make a difference.)

Case study: Brainstorming

One problem faced by LPT, a European engineering distributor, was its diverse work force in ten different countries. The Human Resources Director wanted a way of reinforcing the 'one brand' image. A brainstorming session was conducted with senior managers and country representatives.

83 items were listed. The items were voted upon and the shortlist of 3 items was turned into actions through a project management approach (see T&T No 22).

These were:
i)   Consistent buying and selling policy and procedure.
ii)   Consistent induction process for all new staff.
iii) A multilingual e-learning training package to ensure all staff are aware of what the company does.

This last item was one of the last ideas put forward during the brainstorming. Their e-learning package is now seen as an element of advantage over the companies' competitors.

T&T No:	41		
Title:	CREATIVE AND LATERAL THINKING		
For use by:	Anyone		
When to use:	When seeking alternatives or a competitive edge		
Also see T&T No:	20, 22, 40		
Difficulty Rating:	2	Category:	(F) Creative Techniques

Creative and Lateral Thinking

Key points

- Creative thinking is an important part of problem-solving (see T&T No 20) and can be used in any part of the Project Way of Working (see T&T No 22).
- 'Creativity is that moment of clarity when we look at a problem from a different angle and discover a solution'.
- ☀ Creative thinking is all about making connections that other people don't make.
- As managers, we need to apply creative thinking techniques, not just as a tool to pass on to others, but also for continually thinking how we ourselves can improve the way we manage.
- The more creative we are, the more creative others will be. We need to show the way.

Lateral thinking

Lateral thinking is when we are able to make a connection between two or more ideas or concepts which have no obvious link. How is it done?

👥

Step 1   Ask: 'What (or why) is this important (to you/us)? 'What is this an example of?' Or 'For what purpose?' Or 'What are the main themes/issues here?' Or 'What's the thinking behind this?'

Step 2   Ask: 'What other/similar types/situations are there?'
Step 3   Ask: 'What specifically?' Or 'What are some examples of this?'

Synergy

◀᎐ The combination of two or more qualities or ideas to create something new. Creative and lateral thinking; sometimes referred to as 'Blue Sky' thinking or 'Out of the Box' thinking are important qualities for any team or organisation if they wish to adapt to continually increasing customer or consumer expectations. It is also useful to challenge what sometimes can be seen as an intractable problem.

How?

Take time out, surround yourself with unusual designs and colours. Choose an environment out of the work situation. Give yourselves permission to 'go wild' with your ideas – do not judge others' contributions. Build on them. Have fun, tap into your child-like imagination that is often suppressed – go for it! (See T&T No 40.)

What is lateral thinking?

Lateral thinking is a means of achieving creative thought by extending the thinking process beyond its normal limits.

When to use it

Lateral thinking is best used as part of the Brainstorming process in:
- Developing visions or desirable outcomes.
- Developing possible solutions.
- Developing action plans.

What does it achieve?

Lateral thinking encourages the breakdown of barriers which inhibit creative thinking. We normally limit our thinking by what has been before, or by staying within the boundaries of our present situation – i.e. 'tramline' thinking or 'tunnel vision'. It is important to 'step outside' this routine thinking and be able to generate ideas not constrained by past or present practices and attitudes.

Key steps

- Breaking down the 'No' barrier.
- Challenging accepted outlooks/statements.
- Dr Edward De Bono's Six Thinking Hats can be useful to guide people's thinking in a particular way to suit the type of thinking needed.

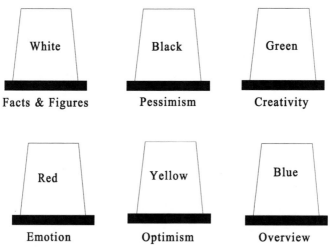

| White | Black | Green |
| Facts & Figures | Pessimism | Creativity |

| Red | Yellow | Blue |
| Emotion | Optimism | Overview |

✒ By making explicit the type of thinking required for any given type of discussion, you help focus people's attention, giving them permission to be free in their thinking. This is particularly important for creative/lateral thinking (sometimes referred to as 'right brain' thinking which usually contains more emotive, creative content than logical, rational or 'left brain' thinking.)

Case study: Creative and Lateral Thinking

There are at least 54 uses for a paper clip!

When starting a meeting that requires free flow of ideas with creative output or lateral thinking, I will start with a warm up exercise to get people into that type of thinking mode. Sometimes, people need permission to be creative.

Another illustration or exercise I use is the 'shrinking rope' problem. Place two rope circles on the floor – one 65cm in diameter, the second 35cm in diameter.

The task, for a group of 5 or 6 people, is for them together, all at once, to put one foot into the rope circle with the other foot off the ground.

You give them the instruction and demonstrate, whilst stood up, using the 65cm Ø rope.

The real challenge is to apply the same rules to the 35cm Ø rope circle, repeating the instructions and demonstration – your foot, of course, barely fitting inside the 35cm Ø rope circle.

The group have great fun holding on and hugging each other to achieve the task in the 65cm Ø circle, but it's amazing how long they will attempt to do exactly the same thing in the smaller circle. Until someone says – 'there must be another way!'

Groups will fall into the trap of interpreting instruction in one way – and need help to shift their thinking laterally. The solution for this task is found when someone realises that the instruction didn't insist on us standing upright.

Some organisations paint rooms certain colours (de Bono colours) to encourage particular types of thinking. I certainly will not run a workshop or hold a long meeting in a room without daylight. The physical working environment can make a significant difference in the quality of thinking.

T&T No:	42		
Title:	RICH PICTURING		
For use by:	Facilitators, Team Leaders		
When to use:	Team involvement in a shared understanding of what's going on		
Also see T&T No:	40		
Difficulty Rating:	3	Category:	(F) Creative Techniques

Rich Picturing

What is it?

A 'rich picture' is a way of summarising everything that is currently known about a situation. It will contain two types of information.

Firstly, it contains 'hard' information; which means the factual data relating to the situation.

Secondly, it contains 'soft' information; this is basically everything which does not fall into the 'hard' category. This may include the perceptions of the people involved in the situation; hunches, guesses and so on. In short; all the subjective data which has a bearing on the problem, situation or issue being reviewed.

Rich picturing is the process of creating a pictorial representation of an organisation or situation, using agreed symbols to represent people, places, problems, feelings and general issues.

It is 'the expression of a problem situation compiled by an investigator, often by examining elements of structure, elements of process, and the situation climate' (Checkland, P., 1981).

When to use it

1. At the start of an improvement project, when trying to get a feel for the scope and size of the problem.
2. When generating the 'preferred situation' or vision, the subjective elements of rich picturing may prove helpful in generating the 'how would it look' scenario.

It is useful at the beginning of a meeting, conference, seminar or time-out to initiate discussion and to establish an overview of the positives and negatives of the situation under discussion. It may be useful as a non-threatening approach to addressing a difficult situation.

What does it achieve?

Rich picturing provides a way of representing the situation as a whole. It gives something from which you can stand back and attempt to see the situation at a glance. It cannot be done with text, because text is linear and sequential, whereas a picture may be 'read' at random. It may also show patterns and arrangements which would be impossible to see from a written description. A rich picture creates a shareable representation of a situation.

Key steps

1. Be clear and have a common understanding of the problem being worked on.
2. Look for the elements of structure in the situation, such as connections, hierarchy, or relationships.
3. Look for the elements of process in the situation, such as sequence, movements, or events.
4. Look for the climate of the situation in the feelings of others and the working atmosphere.
5. What are the subjective elements of the situation? Hunches, guesses and questions.
6. Add everything else that you feel is relevant.
7. Be prepared to use pictures, not words! Give permission to be creative, using colour and any other materials that may help to tell the story.
8. Appoint an artist.
9. Brainstorm and identify symbols. (See T&T No 40.)
10. ☐ The artist will draw agreed symbols on flipchart.
11. ☐ Appoint a scribe.
12. The facilitator will ask key questions to instigate the placing of symbols on the large sheet of paper by the participants.

13. The scribe will write positive and negative points on flipchart as they occur during discussion.
14. When it is finished, stand back and reflect on it. Look for new perspectives and look for links or groupings.

Time required

This can vary according to the size of the group and the complexity of the issues under consideration. Within small groups (of fewer than 6 people) one hour would be sufficient. In larger groups, the session can extend to fill half a day and may require splitting into workable groups to ensure everyone gets a chance to contribute.

Resources required

1. A Facilitator or appointed leader/supervisor.
2. Commitment and co-operation from all participants.
3. Large sheet of paper (several flipchart sheets taped together),
4. Large coloured pens and materials (sometimes, magazines for cutting out images can be powerful – use scissors and glue).
5. Flipcharts.

Detailed instructions

The participants should be seated in a circle, around a large sheet of paper and a supply of coloured marker pens placed on the floor nearby. The facilitator should start with a brief explanation of the purpose of the session and the principles of rich picturing.

An artist is appointed and the group then brainstorms ideas for pictorial symbols that represent various issues, attitudes, feelings, people, places etc contained within a problem situation. The artist draws these agreed symbols on a flipchart, which is left on display to refer to throughout the discussion. More symbols can be added as they occur during the session.

A scribe is appointed and stands, with a flipchart, at one end of the room. The coordinator/facilitator then asks a series of key questions and invites participants to draw their answers on the large sheet of paper, using the agreed symbols rather than words. Opportunity should be given for participants to explain to the group why they have used a particular symbol and what it represents to them. The coordinator/facilitator should keep the discussion going by asking questions and should encourage all members of the group to join in.

As positive and negative points arise, the scribe should note them down on the flipchart in order that key issues are captured and can be further examined and discussed.

Illustrations and examples

The rich picturing technique can be used to identify points and stimulate discussion about issues that are relevant to a particular department or group of staff.

Examples of symbols

☺ Feeling happy about something
☹ Feeling bad about something
☎ Communication
💣 Potentially explosive situation
⧗ Not enough time
→ Lines of communication
🖥 Information technology

Examples of key questions

1. The whole sheet of paper represents the organisation.
    a) Plot the sites, the geography.
    b) Plot your department in relation to the organisation.
    c) Plot yourself in relation to the department.

2. Draw in lines of communication:
    a) Between sites.
    b) Between functions within your department.
    c) Between individual people.

3. Draw a symbol for the site at which you work – how does it feel to be here?

4. What issues are around that prevent you from carrying out your role effectively?
   a) Relationships/communication with management.
   b) Conflict.
   c) Information technology.
   d) Excess workload.
   Use symbols to represent these issues.

5. Using the agreed symbols, represent issues which
   a) are good and positive.
   b) could be improved.
   c) could, if implemented, improve the situation.

Finally

This should be fun – don't be too logical or controlled over the process. It can be messy, but this is likely to reflect the reality of the situation described.

T&T No:	43		
Title:	CAREER COUNSELLING FOR MANAGERS		
For use by:	Managers with Staff		
When to use:	Review of staff performance/progress		
Also see T&T No:	17, 40, 42, 44		
Difficulty Rating:	5	Category:	(G) People Development

Career Counselling for Managers

A common counselling situation that a manager is confronted with is when a member of his staff begins to talk around his present 'job status'. Some of the common themes that occur are often in the context of a general 'chat' or in relation to an appraisal, such as:

- 'I'm not sure where I'm going from here.'
- 'I'm happy at what I'm doing but wonder if there is something else.'
- 'All this change, I don't know what's expected of me anymore – the future looks bleak.'
- 'There's so much change going on and so many opportunities, it makes me feel that I'm standing still.'
- 'I've a choice; redundancy, relocation or redevelopment – some choice!'
- 'Because of our unit/team changing its function, I'm not sure I fit anymore.'

At this point, it is important for the manager to listen and understand, before helping explore what the options and career steps may be.

Here are some self-assessment questions to explore your own career ambitions (these can also be offered to staff in preparation for a career conversation):-

- ☐ What opening statement would you make about your job situation?
- Write down other themes, statements that you have heard about what's going on in your own team or department.

A career/development counselling session can also be prompted by the manager – for example, asking:

- 'Given your present work situation, how do you feel about your prospects?'
- 'Where do you see yourself in two years time?'
- 'What would be different in two years time compared with now?'

These series of questions go quickly from present to future orientation, focused toward helping the employee consider his/her own development. This should lead back to present thoughts and feelings, working toward clarification of the situation and helping the individual discover new insights and options.

Stage 1: Telling the story

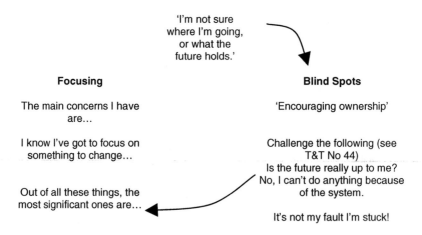

Having helped clarify his/her position in terms of concerns, dissatisfaction or indeed confidence and enthusiasm, then it is appropriate to help build the desired future picture.

Often, individuals narrow down their options because of previously chosen career paths, or because of what is established practice – e.g. 'I need to be in this position for 2 years before I can apply for promotion' – or indeed by looking at what is available before first considering what it is they want.

Stage 2

This part of the model is key to freeing imagination and opening up options. What helps here is not to specify positions of jobs, but to describe what the position would be like, what would it involve – for example...

Future Picture

> More responsibility. Working more with people, flexible hours, variety in tasks, more time for my own development ......etc, etc

☛ Note: status and money are not part of this particular picture. It is often the case that to achieve this sort of future, individuals tend to assume that promotion of some nature is necessary. However, many development plans can focus on changing self and the present situation or involve a lateral move, all aimed at improving the quality of working life.

The next two steps help focus on what is realistic and to look at his/her commitments, for example as indicated in the following diagram:

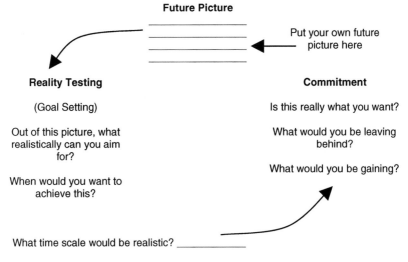

Future Picture

Put your own future picture here

Reality Testing

(Goal Setting)

Out of this picture, what realistically can you aim for?

When would you want to achieve this?

What time scale would be realistic? _____

Commitment

Is this really what you want?

What would you be leaving behind?

What would you be gaining?

This whole phase often lends itself to further exploration of the present situation and the future picture.

Stage 3

At this point it is usual for someone to already have some ideas, action towards meeting the desired picture. The following stages help build up a 'rich' variation of methods paths and actions that the person could take – for example, by brainstorming using the prompts (see T&T No 40), work towards opening up options in order for the employee to choose an effective plan. The following is a list generated by someone who wanted to achieve a similar picture to the one shown in Stage 2 on page 183:-

- List the things I think I'm capable of and making them visible.
- Delegate my routine tasks to leave space for taking on more challenging things.
- Draw up a timetable on certain tasks to ensure a core responsibility – thus increasing likelihood of flexi-time.
- Liaise with other groups to seek the possibility of involving myself with other training programmes.
- Talk to X regarding the possibility of working with him on a project.
- Enquire about vacancies in Y group or enquire about the possibility of experience with them on a temporary nature.
- Advertise myself and see what feedback I get.
- Begin to do things I don't like doing and handle the consequences.

There were others. From this list help in formulating a specific action plan is needed, such as:

- What are you going to do first?
- What seems most significant?
- What is realistic?
- Which of these is most likely to help you achieve your picture?
- What is the likely effect of you doing this?
- Are you able to do it? Have you the resource, including time, ability and support?

These series of questions lead into the final stage of looking at specific action statements and helping the person increase his/her likelihood of success by avoiding inertia (no start) and entropy (fall apart).

The following question series help the above (taken from T&T No 17 – Force Field Analysis):-

- What's going to help you do this?   → helping factors
- What's going to get in the way?   → hindering factors
- What will increase the effect of the helping factors?
- What will decrease the effect of the hindering factors?

At this time, the whole question of support is explored and also issues such as progress review and the nature of support required from the manager is handled at this time.

✒ The above is meant as a guide only. Often in career/development counselling sessions the issues of

- motivation
- adaptability
- suitability for the job
- consequences of change
- domestic situation
- present work relationships

make this potentially to be a complex and difficult process. Hence the need to maintain the qualities and skills of counselling throughout the situation in order to increase the likelihood of developing an effective personal action plan for his/her own development.

(Adapted from Gerard Egan, *The Skilled Helper A Systematic Approach to Effective Helping*, 4th Edition, 1990.)

◄◗ **Warning.** When considering career options, it's important to be realistic in terms of job opportunities within the organisation. Lateral moves maybe satisfying and considered a career move, but most people look toward gaining increase in terms and conditions of employment. Professional help may be needed through designing and running assessment centres or using psychometric tests to find an individual best fit option in career terms.

Case study: Career Counselling for Managers

Jason had just been unsuccessful in gaining promotion and came to me in quite a deflated and demotivated state. We spent 15 minutes exploring his reasoning and understanding why he had failed to impress the interviewers.

There was some recognition that perhaps, at this time, it's for the best as it wasn't exactly what he wanted. The job entailed moving house, family and working in a HR team for a large company. Jason currently worked well in a small team, specialising in 'people skills' training.

Listening to his insight to 'this is perhaps not what I want right now' led me to ask 'ideally, what is it you do want?' We spent a fun 20 minutes creating Jason's ideal work/life balance situation, following which came his reviewed commitment to change. One of his options was freelance consultancy work, which he had not seriously looked at before.

After another few meetings, Jason's plans to become self employed were robust and realistic. He is today a successful consultant in his own right.

T&T No:	44		
Title:	CHALLENGING SKILLS		
For use by:	All staff		
When to use:	When faced with Brickwalls – i.e. resistance to change		
Also see T&T No:	2, 34, 43		
Difficulty Rating:	4	Category:	(G) People Development

Challenging Skills

The following are aspects of how to challenge or positively confront another individual's discrepant or dysfunctional behaviour. These skills are also useful in challenging peoples 'blind spots' or resistance to change, and very importantly – to help them see their own strengths more positively.

The following are important points when preparing for this type of meeting and conducting it using a range of skills and behaviours.

1. What's the 'contract'? Purpose of the meeting?

Do you both agree the agenda?

Can you both agree on the outcome you are looking for? Examples might be:

- A development plan to improve my areas of weaknesses.
- A refocus of my priorities.
- An agreed change in job role that makes best use of my strengths.

It could be that all these are possible and, therefore, at least have an overarching positive intention before a 'challenging' discussion (for example, for the individual to leave the meeting with a new perspective and greater confidence in own development).

2. Earning the right to challenge

✒ This requires you to demonstrate your understanding of the situation from the others' perspective – i.e. empathy.

Actively listening to the story and demonstrating empathy will do this.

It will also enable you to listen for strengths and possible 'discrepancies' between intention and action, or, in other words 'said and done' policy. This can then be one basis for challenge.

3. Your own personal state

Speaking clearly, calmly and with positive intention is important.

Your own reluctance, anxiety and fear should not be evident. (See Reluctance to Challenge in this T&T.)

Remember – the purpose of challenge is for the receiver to gain new insights (see through their blind spots) so that they can adapt new behaviour.

Give the person time to explore new territory – give them permission not to have all the right answers and it's OK to be confused. This is often a pre-cursor to new insight.

4. Ownership

Basic principle – 'You can only change those things that you have some control over'.

Listen out for 'blame' – 'All my problems are as a result of other people, the system, lack of resources, the culture etc.'

The challenge here is to focus on the 'I'. Where are you in all this, what's your issue, your reaction, how are you handling things?

- 'I have difficulty with managing social and political relationships.'
- 'I am not confident in unstructured environments.'
- 'I am unable to think 'big picture' and too narrowly focused on important detail.'

5. Confrontation

This does not refer to 'hitting the issue head on', as this will create further defensiveness and potentially longer term resentment and mistrust.

This does refer to helping the individual identify discrepancies between intention and reality – for example,

- 'On one hand I want to be a strategic and corporate executive, but on the other – all my efforts and actions are in the operations.'
- 'I pride myself in being fit – yet I work 60 hours a week, drink too much and get far too little exercise.'

The nature of these challenges is powerful, hence the importance of building up trust and positive collaboration between you before delivering the message.

6. Advanced empathy or 'playing the hunch'

Sometimes when listening to someone you may realise that something just doesn't quite fit. In certain circumstances you may find that demonstrating to them what you do understand – and then following through on what you don't – can illustrate not only your confusion, but the others' confusion also.

Playing a hunch 'tentatively' could lead to a breakthrough – for example, 'Could it be that something else other than work issues is distracting you at the moment?'

7. Immediacy

Sometimes, when you just don't seem to be getting anywhere and you feel there is an 'atmosphere' between the two of you, then make it 'discussable' – as any couple who wants to make their relationship work would do. The difference here is that you put yourself on the line first. You give the other permission to give you feedback (rather than offer it yourself). To do this you might say, 'We don't seem to be getting very far – is there something I have or haven't done that is creating barriers between us?'

8. Information giving

◀» Basic principle – don't give advice as your first option to be helpful. A word of caution – in critical areas, where an inexperienced manager is struggling, it maybe expedient to offer advice and direct the manager. However, doing this as the norm will suppress personal growth and create dependency and an opportunity to blame the advice-giver if things go wrong. There is a subtle difference between advice giving and information giving. It involves giving facts, examples, references or research relevant to the individual's situation or questions – for example, you might say 'I don't give advice, but what I know from experience is that when you get a high turnover of staff, high sickness rate, negative exit interviews and poor response to job adverts, then it's time to take a serious look at what it's like to work around here and some of your people management policies.'

9. Exploring values

This requires a deeper understanding of the individuals 'drivers' and degree of importance they put on a particular view point or approach.

*   'Why does it have to be like this?'
*   'What's important to you in all this?'
*   'What will you not compromise – why?'
*   'What are you trying to achieve for yourself – how important is this – why?'

These series of questions are powerful. The answer to 'why' is the most difficult one to be clear about and is sometimes useful to let the individual reflect on this for themselves. It is also wise not to start with this – better to explore the situation first.

10. Summarising

This is where you help the other draw together themes or threads that link – focusing on the common denominator which is usually themselves!

11. Feedback

Giving and receiving feedback is often involved in challenging discussions! It can make or break a relationship. Feedback is always challenging whether it's giving it or receiving it.

The principles of *giving* effective feedback are important – i.e. the feedback should be

- evidence-based
- on behaviour
- relevant to the situation and contracted (given permission)
- recent, not ancient history
- in 'chunks' the individuals can take in (not excessive or character assassination)
- given tentatively, with positive intention and support
- followed up with an appreciation and understanding of what impact the feedback has had.

Receiving it?
- Take it as a gift – be non-defensive.
- It's an opportunity to learn how you are seen – at the same time, recognise that someone's perception of you is also a reflection of themselves – so use it for what it is rather than taking it as a personal criticism or put down.

12. Reluctance to challenge

◀▮ This is a very common phenomenon and is related to having the following beliefs or experiences:-

- 'The bearer of bad news' syndrome (may get shot).
- 'Fear of hurting someone's feelings or creating some form of emotional damage.'
- 'Uncovering an area that would be too difficult to handle.'
- 'Reluctance to get close to someone.'
- 'Fear of rejection.'
- 'Wanting to be liked.'
- 'Being rejected or hurt in the past yourself and therefore not wanting to repeat the experience for someone else.'

- 'Can't afford the emotional investment – just too difficult – easier to avoid or ignore.'
- 'Fear of reprisal.'
- 'Fear of breaking friendship or trust.'

All the above are legitimate and understandable reasons for not engaging in challenging conversation – however, they can be dysfunctional.

They may be as a result of witnessing or being on the receiving end of inappropriate challenge from a very early age – family and school experiences are common sources, such as school bullying and/or sibling rivalry not to mention inappropriate parental control methods.

Working through these beliefs and coming to a more positive state or way of perceiving self and others is one area of development – the other is to practise and experience positive challenging behaviour/skills and appreciate that it can be a very rewarding and a 'breakthrough' opportunity to genuinely help another.

Challenging skills – hints and tips

1. Helping individuals recognise what they can and can't influence – encourage the 'I' – ownership.
2. Be a mirror to reflect back the discrepancy between what someone says and does.
3. Listen to the full story and summarise back helping the individual to pick out themes or links.
4. Be prepared to discuss potential barriers between you (immediacy) – talk through 'baggage', ie things in the past that have caused problems.
5. Listen between the lines, observe non-verbal communication – play your hunch (tentatively) that maybe there is something not said – or something else going on.
6. You may need to give some factual information to help someone see things from a different perspective.

Challenging skills – examples of challenging responses

Summarising

Let's look at your last job moves:

1. Dissatisfied with the way you were managed and had little respect for your job.
2. You got a department move because you were in dispute with your boss about appraisal.
3. You left because you felt you were being undervalued.

Themes:
- Managing upwards.
- Consistency between seeing self as others see you.
- Negative career move.

Advanced empathy

You're feeling frustrated because the vacancy you have is one you've agreed is crucial to the operation yet the 'freeze' policy is blocking you. I wonder if there is anything else going on as it's unusual for you to react as if you're helpless here.

Confrontation

You say we are committed to continuous improvement yet when we have a failure or make a mistake we get punished – how does that encourage learning and feedback which is crucial to a continuous improvement culture.

Immediacy

We don't seem to be making much progress, and I don't know for you – but for me I think there is a little defensiveness between us – I'm wondering if how we have worked in the past and the fact that we haven't reviewed that – may be getting in the way.

Information giving

I don't like giving advice – but what I do know is that – if you are on call 24 hours a day, 7 days a week, working weekends and late – and are continuously reacting to the demands of others – something eventually suffers – either your health, your home-life, or both.

I/Ownership

'This consultancy job is tough – Clients won't book time in advance, family gives me grief time I'm away from home, plays havoc with my fitness, and the amount of eating and drinking I have to do is not helping either.'

    Challenging Response – out of this picture you describe, what's within your control that you can potentially change or influence?

T&T No:	45		
Title:	COACHING, MENTORING AND ACTION LEARNING		
For use by:	Supervisors and Managers		
When to use:	To develop your staff		
Also see T&T No:	28, 34, 43, 44, 46		
Difficulty Rating:	4	Category:	(G) People Development

Coaching, Mentoring and Action Learning

Coaching

Coaching is a means of passing on knowledge and supporting others in the development of new skills or behaviours. In doing so, improving overall performance.

The following is a coaching process relevant to helping staff acquire a new skill in competence to perform a particular task:

Coaching process

Input

- Explain/demonstrate the task in hand.
- Identify and explain the key points and important aspects of the procedure.
- Use the 'get-it-rights' to focus your input. Then the person being coached can incorporate these into his/her own style without a loss of quality.

Model/Illustrate

- ✓ Show only the operations or steps required.
- Make sure you do it right, otherwise you are teaching mistakes.

- Do not be tempted to be 'super efficient' or pack so much in that understanding is compromised.
- Go slowly enough for each discreet step or skill to be identified with the learner.

Clarify

- Allow your staff to raise points for clarification, then explain.
- Check for understanding – do not assume that one explanation is always enough.
- If required, get the learner to explain the process to you, and clarify points raised by this.

Do

- Allow your staff to get on with the task, in their own time – or, if needed, with your direct supervision initially, before letting them get on with it.
- Agree a realistic deadline for completion.
- If required, communicate to them when you will be available for support, clarification etc. Then be available.

Review/Feedback

- Reinforce strengths or positive attitudes, behaviour or performance.
- Give feedback on behaviour/performance indicators, not the person's worth or value based on 'failure'.
- Be specific – give specific examples.
- Demonstrate your intention to be helpful.
- ☛ REMEMBER – coaching is a learning process. It is OK to make mistakes.

Step by step coaching process

1. Agree with the staff member the area of the new skill or development.

2. Explain and describe relevant context, theory, background or why this is important.

3. Assess the staff members' degree of motivation and confidence – understand and agree how to work together.

4. Illustrate and demonstrate the new skill/behaviour. Respond to questions and feedback.

5. If necessary, break the task into manageable 'parts' and ask the staff member to do a little at a time– building on success.

6. Give the staff member an opportunity to complete the task. Set an early review point or appointment.

7. Review the performance, highlight what went well, understand why certain mistakes occurred. Agree any new areas or be coached in or reinforced.

Performance coaching

An important aspect of a managers' job is to coach their staff to give them every opportunity to achieve their full potential. The GROW model is a useful framework to plan your coaching conversations. (Ref: Whitmore, J., 2002)

GROW model:

Goal
: Agree what the individual wants to achieve. Explore personal aspirations and focus on specific skills, experience or responsibilities the individual wants to improve on or learn.

Reality
: Understanding the scope of the development needed is important here. Identifying current performance, gaps in ability, understanding or experience is important. This can be a challenging conversation (see T&T No 44) so it is important that feedback on strengths is also given. The manager can then help identify priorities for development that will create the most effective result.

Options
: Having a picture of what optimum performance looks like can be a useful motivator and guide for future monitoring. Describing choices and alternative ways to achieve this improved performance can be a creative challenge to both manager and staff.

Will
: Once agreement as to the best way to change or improve is made, a real test of commitment to act is needed here – i.e. what will be done differently and when? A clear plan of action, agreement as to the type or amount of support needed from the manager and a contract (see T&T No 34) to review progress is the last step in the GROW Model.

Mentoring

Coaching and mentoring

It can be useful to distinguish between coaching and mentoring. Connor and Pokora explore the differences in the table below. Reference: CIPD Jarvis 2004: in *Coaching and Mentoring at Work – Developing Effective Practice*, Connor, M., and Pokora, J., McGraw Hill in association with Open University Press, 2007)

Mentoring	Coaching
Ongoing relationship that can last for a long period of time	Relationship generally has a set duration
More informal and meetings can take place as and when the mentee needs some advice, guidance and support	Generally more structured in nature and meetings are scheduled on a regular basis
More long term and takes a broader view of the person	Short term (sometimes time-bounded) and focused on specific development areas/issues
Mentor is usually more experienced and qualified than the client. Often a senior person in the organisation who can pass on knowledge, experience and open doors to otherwise out-of-reach opportunities	Coaching is generally not performed on the basis that the coach needs to have direct experience of their client's formal occupational role, unless the coaching is specific and skills-focused
Focus is on career and personal development	Focus is generally on development/issues at work
Agenda is set by the client, with the mentor providing support and guidance to prepare them for future roles	The agenda is focused on achieving specific, immediate goals
Mentoring revolves more around developing the mentee professionally	Coaching revolves more around specific development areas/issues

Action learning

Coaching and mentoring can be conducted within a learning structure known as action learning sets (Ref: Revans, R, 1998).

Included here is the summary I use when running management development programmes:-

In summary, action learning brings together small groups of participants with the following intentions:

- To work on and through organisational/individual issues. This is most effective when the commitment is voluntary.
- To work on real problems. Situations in which 'I am part of the problem and the problem is part of me.'
- To work together to check individual perceptions, clarify (and render more manageable) the issue and explore alternatives for action.
- To take action in the light of new insight. Begin to change the situation.
- Bring an account of the consequences back to the group for further shared reflection.
- To focus on learning, not only about the issue being tackled but also on what is being learned about oneself. This is essential to turn developing understanding into learning that can be transferred to other situations.
- To be aware of group processes and develop effective ways of working together.
- To provide the balance of support and challenge that enables each person to manage themselves and others more effectively.

Each group is provided with a facilitator (set adviser) whose role is to help individuals and the group to identify and develop the necessary skills.

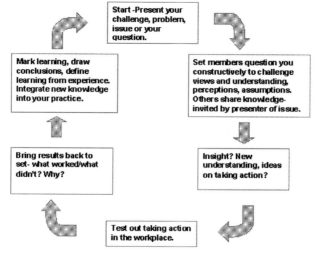

Ref: www.natpact.nhs.uk/cms/316.php

Case study: Skills Coaching

Dylan was a sales manager in a car franchise company. From a recent appraisal, he was told that if he wanted to progress beyond a manager to a 'dealer principal' with increased responsibility for a number of showrooms; he had to improve his presentation skills.

Asking me for help, I first established how he saw his own strengths and weaknesses. I then asked what he wanted in terms of 'presentation performance'. We then set about agreeing a number of coaching sessions.

1. He was to present to me a 5 minute story of how his showroom worked. I used a video camcorder to record this presentation.

    From this, we pulled out the strengths of the presentation and looked at areas he wanted to change.

2. The same presentation was given – this time, I stopped Dylan at various points to reinforce and illustrate the changes he needed to make.

    Following a break, we repeated the exercise with a different topic.

3. I was then invited to his monthly sales team meeting, where he was to brief his team on results, expected targets and news items. Here, Dylan put into practice what he had learnt and our debriefing session afterwards reinforced all the positive aspects, with only a few minor items to work on.

The test was whether his boss noticed the difference – this he did at the next regional meeting where Dylan was congratulated on the quality of his presentation.

T&T No:	46		
Title:	FEEDBACK		
For use by:	All		
When to use:	To improve performance and/or learning		
Also see T&T No:	27, 34, 44, 49		
Difficulty Rating:	4	Category:	(G) People Development

Feedback

Giving and receiving feedback is a fundamental skill for any manager wanting to encourage a continuously improving working environment. Feedback is essential for learning. Many people are fearful of feedback, mainly because of a previous bad experience of receiving it. Feedback should also involve giving positive encouragement, based on highlighting strengths and progress.

Characteristics of effective feedback

- Descriptive, not evaluative.
- Specific, not general, with good, clear, and preferably recent, examples.
- Requested and/or relevant to the situation (Is there a contract? (See T&T No 34.)
- Timing, when receiver is ready – i.e. contracted or asked for – not a surprise!
- Something he/she can do something about.
- Above all, given with the intention to help.

A helpful formula could be:

> What you did/said was . . . .
> It seemed to have the effect of . . . .
> (It made me feel . . . ., because . . . .)

Or

Evidence (observable behaviour)
Effect (it's impact)
Change (to improve) or Continue (build on strengths)

Giving Feedback

HELPING

- Recent examples
- Intend to be helpful
- Describe your own feelings as consequence of other's behaviour
- Be descriptive, non-evaluative
- Specific behaviours: what was said or done
- Reveal your underlying assumption

HINDERING

- Old examples
- General, vague
- Launching in with a factual account without stating an intent to be helpful
- Convey you have a power edge
- Evaluative
- Bring up behaviour that the other can not change
- Fault finding, accusations, blaming
- Attribute negative motives

Receiving Feedback

(It is important as a manager that you model how to receive feedback, thus encouraging your staff and colleagues to give it appropriately)

HELPING

- Request clarification
- Ask for other examples of similar behaviour
- Summarise and feedback what you have heard
- Explore own feelings, record them, of necessary, for reflection at a later date
- Try not to be defensive, listen to understand and be committed to listening
- Check with the individual for validity
- Wait before responding
- Reflect on the meaning of what is being said

HINDERING

- Justifying
- Building a case
- Apologising
- Promising not to do it again
- Getting overly self-critical
- Being judgemental

◀୬ Another persons' perception or experience of you is their reality, however, it is up to you to make sense of it in your own terms, for your own personal development agenda (see T&T No 49).

Case study: Feedback

A lot of my work involves giving feedback to individuals who have a question about themselves at work. This feedback is only effective when the individual concerned is receptive and the moment is right. However, rarely do I need to give my observations as I find it just as effective to ask the individual to explore their own perception about themselves and work out for themselves what alternatives may be better.

It's easy to fall into the trap of giving feedback to someone who says they want it, but are not prepared for the direct challenge. I made the mistake once, by responding to such a request, of conveying my perception of an individual – both in terms of how he came across in a group, but also from what his 'psychometric' profile results were saying – I used the term 'loose cannon'. To this day he refers to himself as the 'loose cannon' and has never really forgiven me for labelling him as such.

Also, trying to make explicit certain dynamics within a group without 'Contracting' (see T&T No 34) with the people concerned by feeding back observations has, to my cost, been quite disabling to the learning process of a particular group.

Therefore, contracting the feedback and working with the individuals' questions is crucial.

T&T No:	47		
Title:	THE JOHARI WINDOW		
For use by:	Team Members		
When to use:	Team building		
Also see T&T No:	44, 46, 50		
Difficulty Rating:	2	Category:	(G) People Development

The Johari Window

Many organisations aspire to be open, transparent and honest; yet in reality, at best they become polite and friendly. At worst, they develop a blame culture.

To develop an 'open' organisation – i.e. demonstrate the value of openness for real – the behaviour of individuals (especially senior management) needs to reflect the ability to give and receive feedback (see T&T No 46) and be willing to disclose appropriately.

The Johari window (see below) can be a useful framework for reviewing the quality of openness in any group or organisation. Originally described by Luft, J., and Ingham, H., (c. 1950, University of California).

SELF

	Things I know	Things I don't know
OTHERS — Things they know	ARENA	BLIND SPOT
OTHERS — Things they don't know	MASK	UNKNOWN

Enlarging the Arena needs TRUST

The Johari Window has four 'panes'. It is based on the principle that of all the things about ourselves that exist to know:

1. Some will be known to ourselves and to other people. This is shared knowledge and is the basis for all of our mutual dealings with one another. Usually called the 'Arena', effective communication is enhanced when we work at maximising the size of this pane.

2. Some will be known to us but not to the people we deal with. Called the 'Mask' or the 'Facade', this is the pane which encourages us to engage in games-playing, trickery, and defensiveness. The larger this pane, the less chance we have of developing truly meaningful and open relationships with others. Elements of this are healthy – i.e. the private and personal sides of our life we choose to keep to ourselves, because it seems irrelevant in a work context. These are our boundaries and need to be respected.

3. Some will be known to others but not to ourselves, this is the 'Blind-spot'. This is potentially self limiting to us because we risk exposing ourselves to weaknesses which we don't know about and which can be exploited by others. (Blind spots can be challenged positively in a supportive environment, see T&T No 44).

4. Some will be unknown to anyone – ourselves and other people. This is the great 'Unknown'. This is a potential source of personal creativity and other resources which we may never have even suspected. Great insight and surprises can be experienced here.

💣 The way to increase the size of the 'arena', while decreasing the size of the other panes is first through self-disclosure (sharing information about the real you with others and thus increasing their knowledge about you) and secondly through obtaining feedback (getting open and honest information about yourself from those who witness you and your performance at work and elsewhere.

The window panes' size will vary, depending on the degree of trust that exists in the group or organisation. The bigger the 'arena' – the greater the degree of trust and the greater the chance of learning.

Case study

I had been working with a personal development group for 2 years now and it seemed to me that we were getting a little stale and complacent in how we were working. I suggested we used the Johari for each of us to gain feedback as to how we were presenting our issues – i.e. the degree of openness and honesty.

We each took our turn – sharing perceptions of each other through drawing different sizes of boxes. For one individual it was particularly challenging, as we all agreed – he was the least open of all of us (i.e. his arena box was small), yet he thought he was the most open.

The discrepancy was explored and eventually, by him disclosing his feelings of inadequacy and insecurity working in the group – he became more relaxed and open.

T&T No:	48		
Title:	LEADERSHIP STYLES		
For use by:	Team Leaders, Managers, Executives		
When to use:	When there is a need to improve direction or motivation		
Also see T&T No:	36, 45		
Difficulty Rating:	4	Category:	(G) People Development

Leadership Styles

Why leadership styles

Although not a tool or technique in its own right, a manager needs to understand how their style of operating impacts on other people. Some self analysis combined with feedback from others can help a manager understand their own personal leadership effectiveness. This section on leadership styles introduces the area and encourages the reader to use the many tools available to help them gain insight to their own leadership development needs. Thus, enabling you to answer the following:-

- What style of leader are you?
- What style of leader is needed in your job/organisation?
- What style of leader do you want to be?

Situational leadership

✪ A good leader will find they adopt a style to suit the current situation. For example, in a crisis or emergency; this requires quick and directive decision-making skills, however, to achieve a task dependant on several people's contributions – this requires a more democratic, delegating/team style of leadership.

A good leader will assess the situation and decide on the basis of:

- Skill levels and experience of the team – the balance between getting the job done in the short term and the opportunity for coaching and self-sufficiency in the longer term.

- The work involved (complex, team development, creative, routine).
- Organisation or business environment (e.g. competitive, changing, at risk or under threat).
- One's own strengths and natural/preferred style of working.

Leadership styles will vary depending upon the degree of supportive and directive behaviours. This can be summarised in the following diagram, adapted from the work of Hersey and Blanchard (1982).

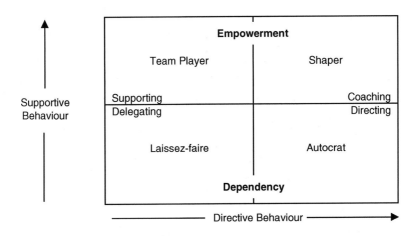

Theory X and theory Y

Leadership styles can be significantly influenced by the leaders' beliefs about the motives of their workforce. This was first described by McGregor, D., (c. 1960) in his Theory X and Theory Y hypothesis:

☛ *Theory X assumptions are that:*

1. Employees are inherently lazy and will avoid work unless forced to do it.
2. Employees have no ambition or desire for responsibility: instead they prefer to be directed and controlled.
3. Employees have no motivation to achieve organisational objectives.
4. Employees are motivated only by physiological and safety needs.

☛ *Theory Y assumptions are that:*

1. Employees find work as natural as play if organisational conditions are appropriate.
2. Employees can be motivated by higher order needs such as ego, autonomy and self-actualisation.
3. Employees seek responsibility since it allows them to satisfy higher order needs.

Effective leaders tend to adopt Theory Y beliefs.

Leadership styles

There are many ways of describing leadership styles, some of the more popular ones are:

Autocratic

High control and high power. Often conveyed by strong egos who have little time for 'bottom up' feedback! Can create a dependent, fearful and resentful workforce. Rarely seen as effective in today's highly modernised and expectant workforce society. However, works well in the armed services and in times of crisis or emergency.

Bureaucratic

Standards, procedures, audit, quality control, laws, rules, regulations, policies and hierarchy. These are the elements and world of a bureaucratic leader. Sometimes appropriate, especially where safety and complex law of finance is involved.

Charismatic

Highly motivating, full of enthusiasm. Often the personality behind a brand which can have value in its own right. Charismatic leaders sometimes run the risk of putting their 'ego' or self image first – taking their 'eye off the ball' or neglecting the basics of organisation performance.

Democratic

The listening leader. Decision-making by majority or consensus. Involves others which enhances motivation and satisfaction. Can involve slow consultative procedures but the end result is often more acceptable than being dictated to.

Laissez faire

Only works when you have a very self-sufficient team and you provide a strategic overview and monitoring role. Can be too 'laid-back' or 'let go' too much – thus resulting in a team lacking direction.

Task versus people-orientated leadership

Extreme task leaders will drive to get the job done, no matter what the cost. Often neglecting or blind to the stress and wellbeing of the staff. The people-orientated leader will work through the feelings and needs of team members with consideration of their talents and wellbeing. The extreme people-orientated leader may run the risk of missing deadlines.

In reality, leaders need a balance of both qualities.

Servant leadership

These people may not have positional leadership, but are seen as influential on the basis that they just quietly and successfully get on with the job.

Transformational leadership

Inspires others, through the communication of a vision, which binds everyone together. Explicit values are expressed and performance of behaviours consistent with their values are rewarded.

Highly visible and put a great emphasis on the importance of communication.

Effective transformational leaders build teams around them, ensuring visionary strategy is translated into pragmatic goals and in turn, are followed through with importance placed on feedback and learning.

A transformational leadership process

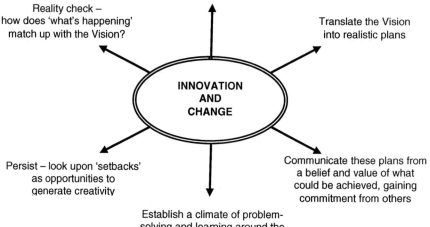

Create a vision describing what it would look like if improved

Reality check – how does 'what's happening' match up with the Vision?

Translate the Vision into realistic plans

INNOVATION AND CHANGE

Persist – look upon 'setbacks' as opportunities to generate creativity

Communicate these plans from a belief and value of what could be achieved, gaining commitment from others

Establish a climate of problem-solving and learning around the plans for improvement

Case study: Leadership Styles

Often at the beginning of management development workshops, I ask 'could the leaders in this group show themselves by putting their hands up?' Usually, after a very poor response, I then ask the same question in a different way – 'surely there must be more leaders here?'   I then get perhaps one or two more hands to rise.   The tentativeness is often accompanied by many in the group looking around, realising that they are not amongst the senior members of the group, so therefore should not consider themselves leaders.

I then confront the situation by explaining the concept of informal –v– formal leadership. Formal leadership may be a position of authority with status and recognised as such in a hierarchy. Informal leadership can be anyone who chooses to positively influence their work situation and the individuals around them.

I then ask 'Are there any informal leaders in the room?' I usually get 100% positive reaction and use this as a basis to reinforce the importance of having 'leadership at every level' within the organisation.

T&T No:	49		
Title:	PERSONAL DEVELOPMENT PLANNING		
For use by:	All		
When to use:	Set your own personal direction		
Also see T&T No:	11, 18, 30, 43		
Difficulty Rating:	2	Category:	(G) People Development

Personal Development Planning

Most people at work want to fulfil their ambitions, realise their potential and have their aspirations and talents recognised. Encouraging personal development planning (PDP's) can give structure to this process and reinforce the importance of individuals taking personal responsibility in managing their own career (see T&T No 43). Managers helping staff review their PDP's can make a significant contribution to the performance management (appraisal) process.

A personal interpretation of Professor Gerard Egan's framework on strategy
(from *Adding Value*, Gerard Egan, April 1993):

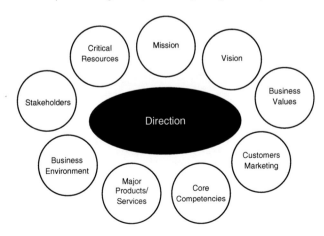

By answering the following questions, you will begin forming a personal development/career plan.

Personal Development Strategy	
Vision	How would I like to be different? What would I like to be capable of doing? What would I like to have achieved? How do I want to be feeling?
Mission	What am I about? What is my purpose? What have I got to offer and to whom?
Values	What are my beliefs? What do I get angry about? What do I care about? What is important to me? What will I not compromise?
Marketing	How can I create opportunities for myself? How do I make myself visible and match what I am capable of with what is needed? How do I express my value and sense of self worth?
Core Competencies	What are my strengths? What is my unique contribution? What reputation do I want for myself?
Product/Service	What range of talents do I currently have? What are my specialities? Which of these do I need to develop? Do my current talents match up with what I want for the future?
Environment	What is going on around me that might influence my life? What changes at work or home might affect my career? What adjustments or trade-offs do I have to make in order to give more time to myself?
Stakeholders	How can I create a support network of people around me and my agenda for change? Who might get in the way and how can I minimise this?
Critical Resources	How am I going to manage my time? What are the conflicting demands? What personal resources do I have that might help me throughout this journey?
Answers to these questions will help form a Personal Development Plan. Setting personal SMARTER goals (see T&T No 18) and gaining support through Career Counselling (see T&T No 43) will increase the changes of you realising your ambitions.	

T&T No:	50		
Title:	MANAGING GROUPS AND TEAMS		
For use by:	Team Leaders		
When to use:	To improve team performance		
Also see T&T No:	51		
Difficulty Rating:	4	Category:	(H) Teamwork

Managing Groups and Teams

To manage a group effectively requires an understanding of how groups develop, behave and the importance of certain key roles.

A group becomes a team when they discover a shared goal that they can all play a part in achieving.

New groups develop into teams by going through various stages. These stages were first described by Bion, W. R., (1961). They are summarised here, with a few additions:

Forming   Uncertainty, nervousness, who's who, polite, nice, formal, sharing expectations, clarifying roles. Apparently willing and getting on with the task.

Norming   Easing into the task, allies, foes and fence sitters are identified. Cliques and social dynamics begin to emerge. Power play begins to show.

Storming   Differences confronted, strengths and weaknesses acknowledged, the un-discussable becomes discussable, challenging purpose and value.

Performing   Energy directed towards the task, results begin to come through. Group learning is high.

Mourning   Task changed or completed. Membership significantly changed. End of group acknowledged – recognition and celebration.

Networking   Group members take experience into different forms, relationships and tasks.

As well as understanding how groups form, in order to shape, control and motivate a group into effective teamwork, the leader or chair will be more effective if they understand 'Content, Interaction, Process'.

These are dynamics that exist in any group, team or meeting at any one time and this is outlined here.

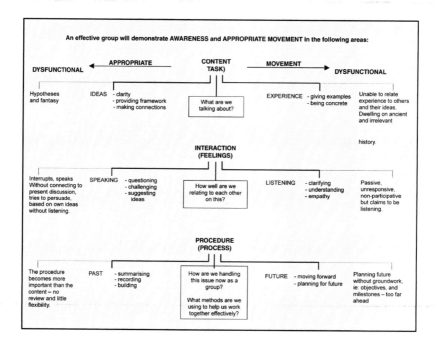

A questionnaire to test out how well we are working together

Any established management team, at some point in time, needs to review their own 'team performance'. This is one way of doing this.

Ask each member of your team to fill in this Questionnaire and then share the results, discussing differences without arguing who is right or wrong.

Questions:	5	4	3	2	1
1. We are working as a team.					
2. There is loyalty to the leader.					
3. Disagreement is dealt with openly.					
4. We pursue priority objectives rather than minor operational and personal objectives.					
5. We make effective use of time in meetings.					
6. We recognise and take pride in team successes.					
7. We encourage positive feelings about our team and our organisation.					
8. We are clearly committed to learning and continuous improvement.					
9. Decisions take account of the need for clarity and consistency. (i.e. fairness with clear criteria)					
10. We ensure decisions are reached on difficult issues.					
11. We action-plan and follow through priority issues, with clear ownership of action items.					
12. We support calculated risk taking.					
13. We fully delegate appropriate decision-making to the next level of management.					
14. We guide others regarding how decisions are to be implemented.					
15. We coach, educate and train our managers.					
16. We reward, recognise and discipline appropriately.					

Rating Scale: 5 = Very Well, 4 = Well, 3 = Adequately, 2 = Not Very Well, 1 = Poorly

DL: www.54.mwauk.com
From 54 Tools and Techniques for Business Excellence, Mike Wash (MB2000)

Managers need realistic expectations of one another, and themselves, in terms of attention to task, team and individual. Adair, J., (1987) model below highlights the importance of keeping all three in balance . In reality, the balance of these activities and their priority will change according to the nature of tasks in a performance orientated world. Managers who are aware of an imbalance can adjust their attention, resources or style of leadership to re-balance.

John Adair's Action-Centred Leadership model is represented by Adair's 'three circles' diagram, which illustrates Adair's three core management responsibilities:

- Achieving the task.
- Managing the team or group.
- Managing individuals.

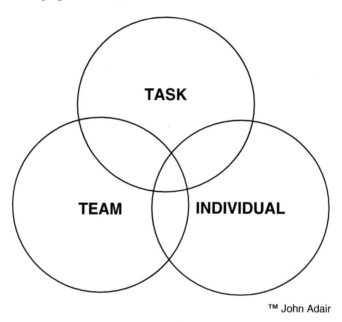

™ John Adair

Case study 1: The Perfect Team

The anticipation of meeting up again was always mixed with excitement and a little anxiety. Excitement because of the potential of us producing something special, the anxiety – well, I guess my own insecurity of wanting to do well and not let anyone down.

Our meeting room is not ideal, yet its limitations dwindle into insignificance once we launch into the task in hand.

The noise levels before we start reflect the frantic catching up with each other, the quick re-establishment of friendships and the exchange of questions and insights about our journey together so far.

We start on time, our leader calling us all together and although we do have one or two people drifting in, they are greeted with recognition that they will be giving themselves a bad time for being late and are quickly integrated with support.

We get down to the task in hand, immediately we fall into role, everyone knowing exactly what's expected of them, and we all have that bit of spare capacity to look around and check if everyone else is OK and clear. In every team there are different levels of ability and in our team, we are blessed with high flyers, yet they are also recognised as equal team members and will readily create a coaching partnership passing on secrets of extraordinary performance to the less able.

Most teams will also develop cliques, and in ours, well they are not so much cliques, but naturally developing sub-groups coming together through age or genuine friendships – these dynamics are used to an advantage, offering additional support to each other and are viewed as a norm, rather than a threat.

We are all clear about the ultimate goal and every time we meet – the goal and vision is colourfully illustrated reminding us of the incentive for giving our best and the ultimate sense of satisfaction we will all feel knowing what we will have achieved.

It's not all plain sailing – there are mistakes. Yet, when this happens, not only the individuals concerned crave to understand why, they also demand feedback so they can learn to improve. These moments can be intense yet the feedback is expressed with sensitivity and skill and everyone pays attention as this moment may offer that gem of learning and insight to help each one of us.

We make rapid progress and the contribution each one makes begins to create a synergy unique to the collective experience and skills we all bring.

We usually meet towards the end of the day, yet even though many of us are tired, sometimes exhausted, the uplift and adrenaline found in us working together dissipates any weariness.

The facilitating skills of our leader are apparent, bringing us in appropriately so our contribution is valued and maximised and each time he offers guidance and direction, we become clearer on how collectively we are progressing toward our goal. Somehow, we simultaneously work at an individual, group and organisational level where, almost by magic, we can be sure the information or resources will be presented in such a way that demonstrates real empathy for what each one of us is trying to achieve.

We develop a form of temporary dependency on each other and with this goes a real sense of responsibility to follow through, and a trust that your team members will do the same.

The smiles are greatest when moments of creative spontaneity produce innovative ideas that make a difference between standard performance and extraordinary performance. Every idea is valued, at the same time; those with experience are well respected, so it's the marriage of differences that create a real sense of special satisfaction.

At the end of our meeting, there's a sense of reluctance to part quickly – almost as if there is some unfinished business – this is often confirmed when we decide to debrief socially and relax together as friends, laughing, joking and already planning together for the next milestone on our journey together toward this single goal that binds us as a team.

Rehearsal night for the UK Premier of
'Titanic – The Musical'
Performed by The York Musical Theatre Company

Case study: 2: The Perfect Job – Teamwork Can Make a Difference

Dick always arrives 30 minutes early for work. This give him chance to catch up with the team, have a coffee, swap stories and get an idea of what the days' challenges will be. Every day is different and each job, although straight forward when first described – to do it to a standard that creates customer delight every time is a worthwhile challenge. Dick is never bored, even in the quiet moments – the team can enjoy the comradeship, review the procedures, attend to the small things that matter but get neglected during the busy times. However, more often than not, Dick is very busy – every minute of the day can be taken up with a customer request, demand, question, observation or just a conversation.

Dick loves this job. He says he is always dealing with happy people and his job is just to keep them that way.

Each team member is clear about what is expected of them and, if needed, are flexible enough to change, at short notice, to suit the overall team performance. The boss is very approachable and occasionally works alongside the team and genuinely wants to hear of any way to improve the ways of working.

When it gets too busy, the team come into their own. They watch out for each other, they cover each others' backs, they fill in the gaps, if someone is struggling, they pick them up. At the end of the day, they share a drink together and pool their tips given by appreciative customers.

Most days, the sun shines and the natural beauty of the workplace is inspirational. The job?

Dick is a meeter and greeter, ranger and starter on the Disney Golf Courses, Kissimmee, Florida.

T&T No:	51		
Title:	EFFECTIVE MEETING MANAGEMENT		
For use by:	Chairpersons		
When to use:	To improve the efficiency of meetings		
Also see T&T No:	39, 50		
Difficulty Rating:	3	Category:	(H) Teamwork

Effective Meeting Management

The following guidelines are offered here to enable good agenda design principles to be applied in the preparation and conduct of meetings.

A meeting is the most expensive way of communicating, problem-solving and/or making decisions in terms of the time spent in them. It therefore seems reasonable that we do the utmost to ensure that the preparation, design and conduct of these meetings are appropriate and successful.

Herewith are the following:

1. Some common practices of the 'not so successful' meeting.
2. A template for aiding the design of agendas.
3. Descriptions supporting the sections within the template.
4. Examples of meetings previously held using the template.
5. Meeting Effectiveness Assessment Questionnaire.

◀» Some common practices of the 'not so successful' meeting

- Chairperson dominates rather than facilitates.
- Use of documents – reading and participation.
- Lengthy discussion with unclear purpose.
- Problem-solving rather than information gathering.
- Structure stifles freedom to contribute.
- Chairperson takes minutes.
- Minutes too detailed, actions not clear.

- Insufficient notice to prepare for a meeting.
- Starting and finishing too late.
- Meeting too long.
- Agenda not varied.
- Individuals unclear about what is expected of them.
- Meeting purpose not clear.
- Domination by one or two individuals.
- Pet and emotive subjects dominate (e.g. cars, pay, car-parking, unions, personalities and the media).
- Difference between strategic and operational discussion is not understood.

If the above describes how your meetings are conducted, then one of the best ways to improve efficiency, time management and communication is to invest in training your managers in meeting skills, the principles of which are described here.

Meeting Management Proforma
(A template for aiding the design of agendas)

Meeting: _____

Venue: _____

Time	Title	Purpose and/or Outcome	Process	Owner	Preparation	Action

Effective meeting management: Descriptions supporting the sections within the template

Meeting

Give the meeting an identity that is clear. It's amazing how many steering groups, directors and operations meetings there are.

Venue

How many of us have turned up at the wrong place or are rushing around asking where the meeting is at the last minute?

Role clarification

The contract between chairperson and facilitator (if present) is usually clarified well beforehand whilst designing the agenda. Other roles such as minute or note taker and presenters are all part of preparing the ground.

Time

Start and finish time needs to be clear and promptly adhered to otherwise significant waste (cost) is incurred waiting for people to start and if finish times are not stated or adhered to then time management and planning for everything else is affected.

Timing agenda items

This is one of the most difficult aspects. It challenges the person who is putting the agenda together to think through clearly exactly what this is trying to achieve and how it will be managed during the meeting. It also communicates to the rest of the group the degree of debate or emphasis the agenda item warrants from the owners perception.

The timings are usually an indicator only and some flexibility is usually called for.

Title (agenda items)

Clarify identity of the topic by Name.

Purpose

State why the agenda item is on – for example, it might be:

- to agree.
- to discuss/debate.
- to give information.

- to identify causes of particular problems.
- to gain ownership/commitment.
- to increase understanding.
- to take stock of progress.
- to develop plans/thinking.
- to introduce new ideas/concepts.
- to propose new policy/project.

Owner   One or two persons' initials needs to be against each item to indicate who has greatest stake or vested interest in this item being discussed. They may also be the person to lead the discussion.

Process   The most neglected area in agenda design. Most agendas consist of lists of items for discussion. This section invites agenda designers to very the way agenda items are handled, thus respecting the fact that most of us have an optimum attention span of 40 minutes and need to do something different if our concentration is going to be 100%. Many meetings are organised for more than 2 hours, this probably means that key decisions are made when individuals are at their least effective. There must be other ways to achieve the purpose of an agenda item, other than information giving and/or discussion – some could include:

- Brainstorm.
- Cause and Effect Analysis (or use some other technique).
- Presentation.
- Small group discussion and present back.
- Individual reflection and present back with a question.
- Brainstorm questions and choose top/critical three.
- Feedback key issues from individuals.
- Pre-reading of relevant papers.
- Structured problem-solving.
- Open negotiation.

...and I am sure there are many other creative ways of getting peoples contribution and participation.

Outcome	This can also be useful, particularly if one of the agenda items is broad or complex. Focusing down on what is expected in terms of the following:-
	• Decision about…
	• Problem solved about…
	• Clarity about…
	This aspect is often left to the chairperson to summarise as the meeting progresses in terms of 'has the purpose been achieved and what is the related action'.
Preparation	This is useful, especially if pre-reading of relevant papers is required. It is very difficult to read and do justice to a paper presented during a meeting. Also, by encouraging individuals to think about each item, they can then come prepared to contribute or offer relevant data/information they have gathered before the meeting. It does require the agenda to be sent out with sufficient time for meeting members to consider.
Action	This section can be left blank and offered as a section for individuals to record action related to each item as the meeting progresses.
Review of meeting	Using new techniques and developing a learning organisation are both important aspects of Continuous Quality Improvement. Feedback can occur for each meeting if a standing item for say 10–15 minutes at the end focusing on how well the meeting went (see T&T No 50), in terms of;

a) Content – did we achieve our objectives and stick to the agenda?
b) Interaction – how well did we listen, question and participate?
c) Process – how well was it chaired and/or facilitated? Did the agenda format work and are there any other ways we could improve the way we meet?

Performance review Periodically, it will be important for established working groups and committees to review their terms of reference and objectives. Checking their performance to ensure alignment with organisation/business need will help ensure the meeting avoids being a drain on resources in a fast changing environment.

The following is an agenda design for a top team in preparation for leading a management development programme. Meetings that last more than one hour (in this case, 4 hours) need to have creative design options in order to maintain optimum attention.

Top Team Meeting
to enable design for Management Development Programme

Venue: Conference Suite
Date: 1st February – 1350 to 1800

Time	Title	Purpose/Outcome	Process	Owner	Preparation
1350	Optimum Working Climate	To shape up and agree the working climate	Group brainstorm – loosely clarifying the meaning of climate in terms of behaviours and skills, values, qualities, etc.	MW	Team members think about what optimum work climate means to them
1410	Ron's Presentation	To consolidate on previous exercise and introduce rationale/focus	PowerPoint presentation:- Q&A – discussion re – shape/change/suitable to present to participants – what else may they appreciate learning?	RM	Ensure Projector and Screen set up (link to lap top)
1430	The MDP	To give an overview of the whole programme	Present the outline and explain the key elements	MW	Prepare a time line overview
1500	BREAK				Refreshments
1530	A model for change and problem-solving	To introduce Model as the foundation for shaping approach and skills	Presentation and discussion		Bring appropriate handouts

227

1600	Mentoring	To clarify the top team role in MDP + short input on listening and feedback skills	Model negative mentoring. Model positive + propose list of key questions to ask before, during and after the programme.	GH MW	Review any of your teams existing personal development plans
1645	Leadership	To outline and experience the MDP Leadership input	Introduce leadership behaviour to skills profile then on to the self & other questionnaire	GH MW RM	Reflect on your own leadership style and its effectiveness
1730	Team Work	To review results of Questionnaire	Give out results – review in context of how this team works.	MW	Complete your questionnaire and send results
1800	Review/Finish	To discuss any issues /concerns/hopes	Open forum.	GH	

To review your meetings, get each member to fill in the following questionnaire. Collate the results, compare and discuss different perceptions – then agree key areas for improvement.

Questionnaire

	The Effectiveness of our Meetings	1 Strongly Disagree	2 Disagree	3 Agree	4 Strongly Agree
1	Our meetings start and finish on time.				
2	The agenda is sent out in good time.				
3	I have ample opportunity to influence the agenda.				
4	Each agenda item is timed.				
5	We give sufficient time to each agenda item.				
6	The meeting is one where my views are welcomed.				
7	I have no problems challenging a member of the group.				
8	My views are listened to and respected.				
9	I participate freely and equally.				
10	Questions are open with very few hidden agendas.				
11	I am confident the whole picture is given when appropriate.				
12	There is very little holding back in our meetings. We say what we think.				
13	We are good at bottoming issues out.				
14	I am clear about how we make decisions.				
15	When needed, we are able to make decisions by consensus.				

The Effectiveness of our Meetings	1 Strongly Disagree	2 Disagree	3 Agree	4 Strongly Agree
16	I am relaxed and confident during the meetings.				
17	I look forward to our meetings.				
18	Action points are summarised and agreed either during or at the end of our meetings.				
19	The minutes are an accurate record of the meeting.				
20	The chairman helps the group to keep on relevant issues.				
21	Conflict is managed well.				
22	There is appropriate contribution from everyone, without domination from 1 or 2.				
23	We meet frequently enough.				
24	Our meetings are long enough.				
25	I am clear about the role of each group member.				
26	I am clear about what is expected of me in each meeting.				
27	The proportion of time we spend on strategic and operational issues is appropriate.				

DL: www.54.mwauk.com
From 54 Tools and Techniques for Business Excellence, Mike Wash (MB2000)

Case study: Effective Meeting Design and Management

Within the first week of taking on a new job, I began to realise a significant mistake had been to give my diary to my new secretary without any brief as to what I wanted or needed.

My job was to develop or improve the whole organisation. A Teaching Hospital with 7,500 staff. My reputation had come before me and it had leaked out that I had a track record of coming from organisations that had significantly downsized.

After a few days of touring the various departments, I was handed my schedule for the following week. Every day was back to back meetings. When I asked my secretary what these meetings were – she replied 'I don't know – people just want to see you – so I have given them all a half hour slot – unless they asked for more!'

I asked my secretary to phone each person who had requested a meeting and ask them: 'What do you want to achieve in the meeting and can you let me know what would be in place at the end of the meeting that's not already there?'

Some replies were very focused and challenging and began to inform me of what my immediate agenda (my job) would look like. 50% cancelled or postponed their meeting – which gave me much more flexibility in terms of who I wanted to meet.

This was the start of changing the meeting culture in this organisation. One of my 'claims to fame' in this organisation was with the Chief Executive at his regular Friday afternoon meeting, which was an open agenda with no finish time. I asked 'When will we finish this meeting?' His reply was 'When I say we are finished.' I then asked – 'but, then how can anyone plan their time for the rest of the afternoon if we don't know how much time we have?' A sharp intake of breath was heard by all!

Fortunately, because I was new into the job, I was able to gain the CEO's confidence and effective meeting management was eventually modelled from the top.

T&T No:	52		
Title:	QUALITY ACTION TEAMS		
For use by:	All		
When to use:	To improve local work situation		
Also see T&T No:	13, 26, 40		
Difficulty Rating:	2	Category:	(H) Teamwork

Quality Action Teams

Imagine an organisation where staff working together took it upon themselves to use brainstorming (see T&T No 40) and Pareto (see T&T No 13) to identify things that they could do to improve their own work situation and/or methods.

Imagine all these staff having already experienced being part of a successful brainstorming exercise, and all understanding what 'the cost of failure' (see T&T No 26) means. What if, as a result of this, they want to immediately apply this experience to improving their own local work situation?

What if some of these teams needed some help and support to get going, to set groundrules and plan ahead, and that this help was available from trained facilitators?

Imagine all managers and supervisors actually creating a work environment where this type of team activity is encouraged.

Quality action teams are small local work related teams, acting on their own initiatives to improve working methods and practices that they have control and responsibility for, such as teams of admin staff sharing facilities or working for the same supervisor, for example.

They are characterised by short meetings, high energy and are action orientated but still respect the key elements of effective problem-solving.

A schedule could look like this:

1. Recognition of the need to improve things – informal conversation and agreement to have a short meeting.

2. First meeting:
   - Set groundrules.
   - Clarify purpose.
   - Brainstorm failure activities (avoid solutions at this stage).
   - Prioritise (3 votes each).
   - There maybe some obvious quick fixes as a result of good quality communication – if so, fine!
   - Commit to go back and gather more information about what's really going on regards priority failure activity.

   (This meeting may take between 30 – 60 minutes.)

3. Second Meeting:
   - Short check – how's it going.
   - What information have we got?
   - What new things have we learned regarding what's contributing to our failure costs/activities?
   - Brainstorm the ideal (the outcome we want either on one specific issue or the full work situation). What should it look like?
   - 'Hold the ideal' – think about, check it out.
   - Talk to other colleagues.

   (Meeting may take 30 to 45 minutes.)

4. Third Meeting:
   - Agree what the team want to achieve.
   - Brainstorm – how many ways can we think of to achieve this.
   - Choose the best ones.
   - Commit to taking first steps – tentatively at first – involving others who may not have been at the meeting.

   (Again – short meeting taking 30 to 45 minutes.)

5. Final Meeting:
   - How's it going?
   - What worked?
   - What hasn't worked?
   - Can we improve things further?
   - What sensibly can we do?
   - Do we need to involve anyone else?

- Do we need help?
- Can we make visible what we have achieved so far and keep going?

(Meeting may take 30 minutes.)

The above description is just one way of managing a Quality Action Team process. Some teams manage to go through the improvement cycle without formal meetings but with a conscious effort during work time, in breaks to:

- identify problems
- clarify ideal outcome
- implement things they can.

Others build the process into established meeting forums.

Essentially, it's giving people permission to take charge of their own improvement agenda and giving this support by providing

- supportive work environment
- tools and techniques
- facilitation, if needed.

Case study: Quality Action Teams

Given a chance, it's amazing what improvements individuals can make to their own work situation when given a little support to work together, and permission to change things.

Seven secretaries who worked in a pool to support the senior managers and academic staff of a college were invited to come together in a quality action team format.

A facilitator helped to create an atmosphere between them where they could, without blame, identify many inefficient and frustrating work practices.

The main problems revolved around lack of team work, suspicions that work was not being divided up equally, favouritism by the management team, confusion over who was responsible for things like car park passes, stationery budget, room booking, even to what seems trivial but a major frustration – the cleaning of the kitchen and making coffee for visitors.

Other problems related to the way work was passed from the academic staff to the secretaries and how some staff insisted on only using certain individuals.

Unreasonable short term requests combined with poor response time to computer breakdown all contributed to a difficult working environment. The relief from the secretaries when all this became discussable was visible on their faces.

After several meetings and a presentation to the senior managers and some key academic staff, roles were clarified and improvements made.

The secretaries decided to meet at least once a fortnight for an hour to check progress, recognising that teamwork in a pool situation was essential for creating a healthy working environment.

T&T No:	53		
Title:	CULTURE CHANGE • 7 Essential Ingredients for successful culture change • Guiding principles and tips for effective culture change • Criteria for successful culture change programme • Guidelines for designing and leading culture change		
For use by:	Managers who want to lead change/Facilitators		
When to use:	When a significant shift in overall organisation performance is needed		
Also see T&T No:	6, 9, 30		
Difficulty Rating:	5	Category:	(I) Total Organisational Change

Culture Change

7 Essential ingredients for successful culture change

(with the aim of achieving a learning organisation culture – i.e. one where continuous quality improvement is the norm)

1. Strategy
2. Commitment
3. Communication
4. New Talent
5. Competency
6. Infrastructure
7. Resources

Steering Culture Change Needs Competent Internal Resources.

1. Strategy

A strategy incorporating visionary elements emphasising values and describing the desired culture in attitude and behavioural terms. This should be set against a clear picture of where the organisation currently stands and a clear statement as to the need for change.

2. Commitment

Firm commitment from the top to this vision measured by the openness to feedback, visible behavioural change and continual improvement through putting personal development plans into action.

3. Communication

Communicating the vision in a style consistent with the desired culture. This includes open, two way briefings, participative discussion and an appropriate style of written communication. Using focus groups, teleconferences and taking full advantage of the technology available today can add richness to any communication plan.

4. New Talent

Select those with the qualities for the future. Induction should reflect the desired culture, not the past.

5. Competency

Competencies and values consistent with the new culture need to be defined. All training should then reinforce these elements of the desired culture. The style of training delivery should also reflect this.

6. Infrastructure

Quality improvement initiatives, whatever their purpose (quality management, quality assurance, clinical audit, risk management, business process re-engineering, customer charter, etc.), should be integrated by a common purpose such as improved efficiency or high quality service) – but just as important, the process to pull these together and implement them should be consistent with the desired culture change. This may need a review of roles and responsibilities, accountability and structure.

7. Resources

A network of trained internal change agents to facilitate and support the shift toward a 'learning organisation' is essential.

Guiding principles and tips for effective culture change

- Must relate to business goals.
- Early winners – need to demonstrate benefits.
- Live out the values.
- Not just top down.
- Needs an implementation team of hand picked people from different levels.
- Clear delineated time scales.
- Recognise that change is frightening – consider support and counselling.
- Capable of demonstrating to the outside world.
- Opportunity to build bridges within the organisation.
- Need to encourage integration of all staff.
- The process of change sufficiently visible to be monitored.
- Installing a new identity.
- Developing a common understanding and language.
- Need to involve the whole organisation.
- Need to be open about how we are developing.
- Need a core development programme for everyone.
- Includes continuous improvement teams, good communication, appropriate use of technology and leadership at all levels.

DL: www.54.mwauk.com
From 54 Tools and Techniques for Business
Excellence, Mike Wash (MB2000)

Criteria for successful culture change programme

- Top Commitment – led by CEO and Directors who practise what they preach.
- Given priority (for example, designed into performance targets of top 20% of managers).
- Robust communication and training strategy.
- Shared understanding of change management and project management by all managers.

- Dedicated people resource to the programme (e.g. a co-ordinator with a trained team of facilitators and/or project leaders).
- Integrated with general training, appraisals and induction in context of HR strategy.
- Hard and soft measures designed and linked to programme activities – e.g. project results in terms of efficiency improvement (hard), staff attitude/relationships survey (soft).
- Explicit description of company vision and values – reinforcing need for a particular style of leadership (highlight skills/competencies).
- Ongoing review of progress, communication and recognition of success.
- A critical mass of managers who take it seriously and embark upon a personal development path which involves reading, research and skills training.

Guidelines for designing and leading culture change

The phased approach is useful in that it helps plan ahead, checks progress and can shape cultures.

In reality, the phases will overlap and within each phase there are complexities and challenges to be addressed, too numerous to detail here.

PHASE ONE
AWARENESS
Top team strength, ambition and awareness

PHASE TWO
PREPARATION
Top team preparation and understanding the implications of culture change and leadership development

PHASE THREE
TRAINING
Top team training, design and prepare for training facilitators and educating all staff

PHASE FOUR
RECRUIT CHAMPIONS
Involve senior managers, select facilitators

PHASE FIVE
BREAKTHROUGH
Train facilitators; put theory into practice to next tier of management

PHASE SIX
INVOLVEMENT
Cascade the process throughout the organisation

PHASE SEVEN
COMMUNICATE AND MEASURE

PHASE EIGHT
CELEBRATE SUCCESS

Phase one. Awareness

Top team strength, ambition and awareness

1. Introduce your ambition for the organisation. This may be 'to be the best' or the need for culture change is borne out of a crisis or a threat. Whatever the reason, it maybe useful to take a measure of the current culture. There are many culture surveys available. One useful resource being www.denisonconsulting.com.
2. Introduce the idea of using frameworks as a vehicle to achieving excellence (e.g. Investors in People (IIP), Scottish & British Quality Award, European Foundation Quality Management).
3. Get the basics right.
4. Pragmatic management – financial control.
5. Find a common language for the top team.
6. Build trust, comradeship and teamwork.
7. Create a vision as part of the overall strategy – sense of direction that key players can buy into, i.e. they can see the benefit or pay off.
8. Put great store in people management – manage the top team performance well and expect them to cascade this.
9. Involve the Chairman and non-execs in an added value role in supporting the strategic agenda.
10. Ask yourself – can this team lead 'transformation'.
11. Bring in data highlighting the percentage of failure activity and its costs.
12. Staff survey/diagnostic.

Phase two. Preparation

Top team preparation and understanding the implications of culture change and leadership development

1. Top team workshop around the question 'How do we create a continuous improvement culture?'
2. Can we develop a learning organisation? (Pedler, M. 1997)
3. They do this by looking at strategy, leadership and team behaviour.
4. They form personal development plans for
   a) personal style, behaviour change and team contribution.
   b) increased knowledge about what it will take to lead transformation.
5. Highlight current internal best practice.
6. Work with key influential players – managers and key professionals.
7. Involve them in early thinking – seek their opinions
8. Devise a robust communication strategy.

Phase three. Training

Top team training, design and prepare for training facilitators and educating all staff

1. Design of a culture change process.
2. Basic education for all staff.
3. Process for involving all staff.
4. Change agent or facilitator training.
5. Agree basic tools e.g. project management framework, problem-solving, tools and techniques.
6. Address basic training needs in the top team.
7. Meeting and time management.
8. Problem-solving.
9. Team leadership skills.
10. Further team building needs
11. Top team preparation for launch of culture change.
12. Begin to set up key improvement groups, e.g. communication, appraisal, best practice.
13. Continue to shape up the vision – highlight values and purpose.
14. Ensure key stakeholders are involved.
15. Gain current perceptions from next tier of management

Phase four. Recruit champions

Involve senior managers, select facilitators

1. Senior Management (and Clinicians or other key professionals, such as lawyers, teachers, specialists etc depending on the organisation) involvement.
2. Design basic material for all staff.
3. Select facilitators and design training.
4. EITHER presentations/briefing from CEO followed by Workshops
   OR workshops led by CEO and Directors.
   OR BOTH.
5. Identify steering group if it's not the top team.
6. Follow up workshops – identify what will work in own unit/dept/function.

Phase five. Breakthrough

Train facilitators; put theory into practice to next tier of management

1. Train your facilitators.
2. Cascade to next tier of management – mixed groups.
3. Add momentum to current improvement groups.
4. Ensure – survey results are directed toward improvement initiatives.
5. Begin to receive proposals from Directors and Senior Managers as to how the change process could be adapted to work in own 'patch'.

Phase six. Involvement

Cascade the process throughout the organisation

1. Match facilitators with directors' and senior management improvement plans.
2. Design in events to keep the momentum going, such as a Chief Executive Awards scheme, or a special newsletter.
3. Check on integration of the new way of working into induction, appraisal, training, and selection procedures.
4. Design database to capture and communicate progress and learning from the many improvement initiatives and projects.
5. Encourage the cascade supported by senior managers with presentations by CEO and Directors.
6. Form 'bottom-up' quality action teams around local improvement initiatives.

Phase seven. Communicate and measure

Communicate, communicate, communicate!

1. Make the links between tangible improvements and the new way of working.
2. Go for some form of recognition, e.g. National Quality Award.
3. Measure, measure, measure!
4. Transform the way notice boards, displays and walls will look.
5. Ensure that customer/patient feedback is considered when reviewing progress.
6. Encourage benchmarking

Phase eight. Celebrate success

Re-launch the programme e.g.: hold a 'Quality Day'.

1. Get the media involved.
2. Re-survey staff, customers and patients.
3. Market the results!!!
4. Stress the importance of keeping going – this is a continuous journey – not a destination – as you turn one corner, or achieve one milestone the horizon changes – better performance is always possible.

Case study 1: Children Values Drive Culture Change – the Alder Hey success story from dejection to pride

In 2000 there was hardly a headline in the national press that was not condemning Royal Liverpool Children's Hospital (colloquially known as Alder Hey) for retaining children's organs without parent's permission. This resulted in significant change in the practice of gaining consent and the revelation that Alder Hey was not alone in this custom and practice.

Demands for culture change came ringing in from the House of Commons and questions of accountability resulted in the dismissal of a Chief Executive and a non–executive director.

Imagine the demoralising effect this period had on all the staff that worked at this internationally renowned children's centre for excellence! Many staff changed their behaviour from proudly saying I work at Alder

Hey to avoiding the subject of work at all as they were often in fear of being over heard by angry, grieving parents.

The job we had to do was tantamount to several mountains to climb:

- Listen and respond sensitively to all parents concerned.
- Manage the legal implications and demands.
- Respond to political and media pressures.
- Continue running the Hospital .
- Maintain staff moral.
- Manage the disciplinary issues and change in practice.
- Somehow keep our heads up – remind ourselves of the excellent work we were doing.
- Start to look forward – rekindle our pride and involve everyone in becoming once more known for being the centre for excellence for specialist children's services.

It's at this latter point where I was called in as a specialist in organisation development. They needed help to recognise the importance of values in the context of a whole systems approach to change.

Introducing the prospect of change in any organisation will be met with resistance – it was particularly important for me to help them present this change without connotations of blame for what had gone wrong, to present it in such a way that builds on the excellent work in place and to encourage everyone to think differently and consider that perhaps there maybe a better way of doing what is current practice in all areas and at every level.

The starting place was at the top. This was going to be a long haul that needed the full support of the Board. A strategic review was conducted taking stock of current performance with a SWOT analysis and then I conducted an exercise that helped them be explicit about vision and values. This, no doubt, is something all organisations do at some time – the difference for them was the recognition of the emotional investment had taken its toll and they had to some how re-energise and look forward.

I facilitated several workshops that resulted in all Board members committing to leading culture change by personally committing to development and change themselves. These workshops were challenging and emotional however they resulted in a foundation that ensured that any culture change programme would be a strategic priority and integrated into the core business of the Trust.

A mandate to embrace everyone in an organisational wide programme of reform and improvement was achieved. We set about designing the process and infrastructure to make this happen. This was based on the elements that also make up the learning organisation.

This now is a well established concept in theory but few realise the many processes and development activities needed to make this a reality.

The following are some of the events and processes I helped Alder Hey implement over a two year period:

- A full time lead co-ordinator with a half time administrator support 5 co-ordinators who agree to integrate change work in current work roles.
- Change agent training for these co-ordinators.
- Identification of 40 facilitators – trained in change and improvement techniques.
- Networking these change agents and facilitators into a learning network using action learning as a model of support.
- Creating an identity for the programme consistent with its aspirations (referred to as the Excellence through Learning Programme).
- Design of a tool kit for facilitators and mangers to use in the context of making improvements.
- Development of a consistent approach to project management and training all facilitators and project leaders in the technique.
- Design of a project database to record and monitor the many improvement activities.
- Making explicit the values and how they link to Clinical Governance and Culture Change.
- Training co-ordinators and facilitators in workshop/training techniques so they can train and involve the rest of the 2500 staff.
- Ensuring a communication strategy well designed and executed.
- A steering group to ensure priorities are addressed and the programme is continually designed and adapted to suit local circumstances.
- Facilitator conferences to keep the momentum going.
- Action teams for excellence developed at every level.
- Integrated strategy for development, ensuring links are made between Investors in People, Improving working lives, CHAI improvement objectives, Improving Partnerships for Hospitals, Leadership development and a measurement framework, such as European Foundation for Quality Management.

The above are some of the elements that made up what is now referred to as their Excellence through Learning programme. The style of consultancy offered was one that believes equipping the organisation with its own self sustaining expertise as soon as they are able – hence the ongoing commitment with their own internal learning network meeting in action learning sets.

So, what has all this achieved – apart from being a 3* trust and moving rapidly to Foundation Status? They won the Excellence in Human Resource Management Awards 2006 as 'Overall Winner' and won the 'Organisation Development and Learning' category.

Case study 2: Changing Culture in Health and Service Systems

Managing change was only part of the answer to the following questions from several Chief Executives wanting to significantly improve organisational performance within the UK Health Service:-

- How can we rekindle the pride in this organisation?
- How can we move from being 'middle of the road' to 'best in class'?
- How can we create a single uniform culture out of what are currently diverse and uneasy relationships?
- How can we move the skill set from coping with change to thriving on change?
- How can we break down the professional and departmental barriers?
- How can we achieve leadership at every level, empowering everyone to act in the best interest of patients within the resources available?

The answer to these questions lay in the realm of whole system organisation development.

Few organisations have successfully implemented and sustained a programme of development, leading to recognised best practice.

The common denominator between successful organisations, who manage this whole system change, relates to the design and practice of certain behaviours and processes, linked to a value based leadership agenda.

The theory of managing change effectively is well published in many useful books, articles and techniques and information readily available via the internet.

However, the practice of effective change management, leading to sustained continuous improvement inculcated within the organisation is rarely achieved. This is because the ingredients of emotional ownership, skilled facilitation and process design are at best weak, or at worst missing.

Emotional ownership

The Chief Executive and his executive team need to fully understand and appreciate the implications of an organisation wide change programme. Emotional investment is achieved by each member being trained along with their own facilitators in the skills and practice of facilitation. The rest of the Board (i.e. non-executives) also need to experience the value of change through the practice of effective communication and meeting management; enabling them to have the opportunity of giving insightful support.

The programme needs to be set in strategic context, focused at achieving priorities, targets and sustained continuous improvement. Creative team time-outs for the Board based around this agenda will encourage unique design and ownership of events requiring visible and effectively modelled leadership.

Creating a top team culture which is open, accessible and one that reduces the barriers of status through effective team work and communication is essential. Each member of the executive team (and Chair) becomes a champion and passionate advocate of the ambition to achieve a 'learning organisation' status.

Skilled facilitation

An organisation that learns effectively will improve if there is a critical mass of skills, encouraging behaviours directed to improving effectiveness and efficiency. The skill set required relates to coaching others in effective problem-solving in the context of managing improvement projects. This can be achieved by training between 30 and 50 members of staff from all levels and professions in facilitation skills (for an organisation between 1000 and 3000 staff). The interpersonal skills and process from the Skilled Helper Model (Egan G., *The Skilled Helper – A Problem-Management approach to Helping*, July 1997) can be adapted to a Project Way of Working (Wash M., 1998, MWA (UK) Limited) – see T&T No 42. This can form the basis and practice of empowerment directed towards all staff having the opportunity and freedom to implement improvements at the service of improving patient and staff experiences.

Process design

Developing the organisation requires a systematic planned programme of events uniquely designed to fit the challenges of the day. The programme champions need courage to push the boundaries, try new ways of working and demonstrate creativity in the design of meetings, workshops and new responses to old problems. A phased approach to development (see *Managing Change at Work, 54 Approaches to Brickwall Management*, Wash M., 2006, pp 137–141) will be reassuringly useful to any manager held accountable for investing in what some may say is a leap of faith, and others will resist; quoting many other initiatives launched with passion and enthusiasm in the past, only to fizzle out as another 'flavour of the month'.

This is why it is important that alignment of the following takes place:

- Structure.
- Policy.
- Information systems.
- Training.
- Development.
- Recruitment.
- Induction.
- Performance management.

This needs to be visibly linked and consistent with the values espoused through the 'change programme'.

Today's Health Service is chaotic and challenging – and will remain so. The nature of health care development combined with managing a gigantic complex system means that today's managers not only have to manage change effectively, but must, at times, thrive on chaos. The same can be said for most of the service industry. Thriving on chaos and excelling in business excellence can be achieved by recognising the interconnectedness of everyone's contribution – and realising that learning companionship, and not professional or departmental rivalry, is the answer.

T&T No:	54		
Title:	ORGANISATION DEVELOPMENT PROCESS		
For use by:	Senior Managers, Executives, Facilitators, Change Agents		
When to use:	A need to change the whole organisation		
Also see T&T No:	53		
Difficulty Rating:	5	Category:	(I) Total Organisational Change

Organisation Development Process

What is organisation development?

Organisation development is the introduction of social systems within the organisation. It involves the practice of planned change to bring about significant improvements in organisation effectiveness.

Some definitions:

'Collaborating with organisational leaders and their groups to create systemic change and root-cause problem-solving on behalf of improving productivity and employee satisfaction through improving the human processes through which they get their work done.'

Michael F Broom

'The activity of improving an organisations ability to achieve its goals by using people more effectively.'

A Dictionary of Management

'A system-wide process engaging everyone in the organisation in the pursuit of excellence, whereby all development activities are integrated and explicitly linked to a vision underpinned by organisational values.'

Mike Wash

'Organisation development is a complex strategy intended to change the beliefs, attitudes, values and structure of organisations so that they can better adapt to new technologies, markets, and challenges.'

Warren Bennis

A useful resource for organisational development in local government (although the principles described here can be applied to most organisations) is http://www.webbnet.ltd.uk/files/odpm_locgov_038920.pdf.

Here is an outline development process for achieving 'learning organisation' status. It may be useful for any new leader taking on a turnaround challenge or just wanting to transform the culture (see T&T No 53).

Step 1	Pragmatic	Get the basics right Stop the obvious waste (capital and human) Deal with the urgent Manage core business (clarify or restate purpose)
Step 2	Set Direction	Scan the horizon Assess current and potential ability Set a general direction (Vision) Begin highlighting core values as criteria for making decisions
Step 3	Set Structure	Right people in the right position Clarify decision-making process and levels of accountability Invest resources in improving communication Get the structure working Clarify personal performance measures and process
Step 4	Internal Quality	Inter and Intra-departmental team building Internal custom-supplier matrix mentality Invest in basic systems
Step 5	Equip the Organisation with tools for Continuous Improvement	Train own Change Agents Ensure the Top Team are champions Involving everyone Invest in Developing people
Step 6	Drive for results	Highlight what works Reward learning Encourage measurement Focus your best at the most important
Step 7	Go beyond the ordinary	Encourage creativity, lateral, out of the box solutions Benchmark against the best and be a model of excellence
Step 8	Whole Systems	Shape and influence the wider community Integrate systems Link process Share/pool resources to deliver on cross boundary problems Achieve optimum and efficient administration Review Vision and review structure

The above Steps 1–8 have logic in that each step builds on the preceding one – however, there will be inevitable overlaps and parts of the organisation may be several steps ahead of the other. This should not be problematic as long as there is a critical mass of momentum of change in the same direction. (More than two steps ahead may create internal dissonance and misunderstanding).

♦ The following two illustrations demonstrate the potential complexity of organisation development, hence the importance to have a simple framework and process to hold it all together. These 'mind maps' or 'rich pictures' were an attempt from two organisations to summarise all the elements of organisation development currently in place.

Organisation & Leadership Development Process in Engineering Dept

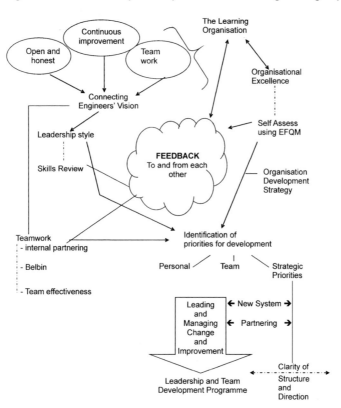

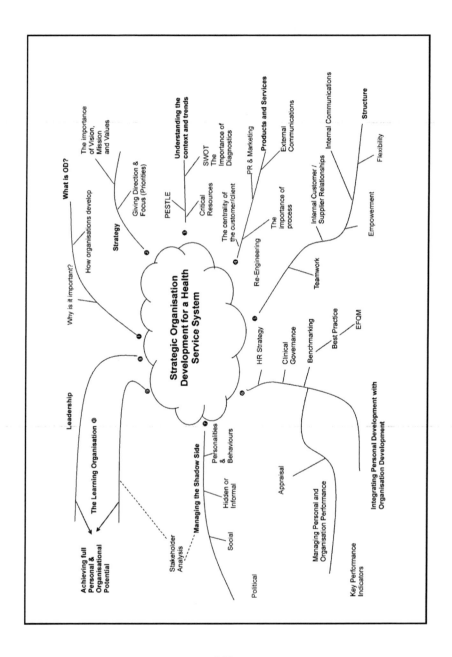

Given the degree of complexity when developing organisations, it is useful to have a framework. This can be used as a checklist to ensure there are no gaps and imbalances and that key processes are aligned with the overall business strategy.

An example of a framework I use in my consultancy is taken from Egan's (1993) Model (Model A: The Pursuit of Excellence Task Cycle) which describes 6 major task elements, within each task there are sub-tasks. These can be a useful guide to ensure elements of organisation development are not missed.

Model A framework

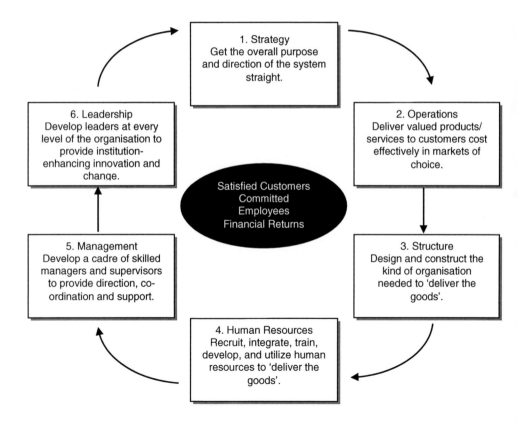

Another popular model is the McKinsey 'Seven S's' framework ref: Rasiel, E., and Friga, P., 2001, which provides a useful framework for analysing the strategic attributes of an organisation. The seven S's are: shared values, structure, systems, style, staff, skills and strategy.

An organisation's 7 S's

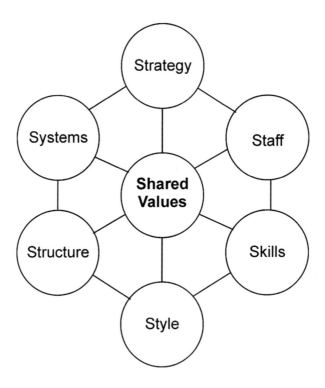

Further Reading

The following books are in my personal library and I recommend any of them to those who wish to pursue business management development and business excellence.

Over the years, I have accumulated a small library of management and organisational development books. Some have stood the test of time and are classics; others bring in current thinking.

I include them here as many are the source of my approach to development and have influenced, indirectly, this book.

For those who wish to explore further the contents of these books, I offer my opinion as to which are:

(L)   Light: easy read, key principles, practical.

(M)   Medium: comprehensive, practical, good mix theory and illustrations of application.

(H)   Heavy: in depth, comprehensive theory, core principles put to the test.

Title	L/M/H	Author	Publisher/Year
Action Centred Leadership	(M)	Adair, John	Gower, 1982
Effective Team Building	(L)	Adair, John	Gower, 1986
Strategy Change and Defensive Routines	(H)	Argyris, Chris	Pitman, 1985
Overcoming Organizational Defences – Facilitating Organization Learning	(H)	Argyris, Chris	Prentice Hall, 1990
On Organizational Learning	(H)	Argyris, Chris	Blackwell, 1992
Knowledge for Action – A guide to overcoming Business to Organizational Change	(H)	Argyris, Chris	Jossey Bass, 1993
Creating Culture Change: The Key to Successful Total Quality Management	(L)	Atkinson, Philip E	IFS Publication, 1987

Title	L/M/H	Author	Publisher/Year
Leaders – The Strategies for Taking Charge	(H)	Bennis, Warren & Nanus, Burt	Harper & Row, 1985
Consultation 2nd Edition – A Handbook for Individual and Organizational Development	(H)	Blake, Robert R & Srycley-Morton, Jane	Scientific Methods, 1963
Managing the Unknown by creating new futures	(M)	Boot, Richard, Lawrence, Jean & Morris, John	McGraw Hill, 1994
The Guru Guide	(M)	Boyett, Joseph & Boyett, Jimmie	Wiley, 1998
Beyond Negotiation	(M)	Carlisle, John A & Parker, Robert C	Wiley, 1991
Moments of Truth	(L)	Carlzon, Jan	Ballinger Pablo, 1987
Systems Thinking, Systems Practice	(H)	Checkland, Peter	Wiley, 1981
Rethinking the Company	(H)	Edited by Clarke, Thomas & Markhouse, Elaine	Pitman, 1994
Coaching and Mentoring at Work – Developing Effective Practice	(M)	Connor, Mary & Pokora, Julia	McGraw Hill in association with Open University Press, 2007
The Game of Work – how to enjoy work as much as play	(H)	Coonradt, Charles A	Shadow Mountain, 1987
Quality without Tears – The Art of Hassle Free Management	(M)	Crosby, Philip B	McGraw Hill, 1984
Corporate Cultures – The rites and rituals of Corporate Life	(M)	Deal, Terrence & Kenny, Allen	Penguin, 1988
Six Thinking Hats	(L)	De Bono, Edward	Penguin, 1985
Alpha Leadership – tools for business leaders who want more from life	(M)	Deering, Anne, Dilts, Robert & Russell, Julian	Wiley, 2002
The Effective Executive	(M)	Drucker, Peter F	Pan Books, 1970
Change Agent Skills in Helping and Human Service Settings	(M)	Egan, Gerard	Brooks/Cole, 1985

Title	L/M/H	Author	Publisher/Year
Change Agent Skills B Managing Innovation and Change	(M)	Egan, Gerard	University Associates, 1988
Adding Value – A Systemic Guide to Business Driven Management and Leadership	(M)	Egan, Gerard	Jossey Bass, 1993
Working the Shadow Side – a guide to positive behind the scenes management	(M)	Egan, Gerard	Jossey Bass, 1994
Managing WITH People	(L)	Fordyce, Jack K & Weil, Raymond	Fordyce/Weil, 1986
Incredible Bosses	(L)	Freemantle, David	McGraw Hill, 1990
A Dictionary of Management	(M)	French, Derek & Saward, Heather	Pan Books, 1984
The Learning Organisation	(L)	Garrat, Bob	Fontana, 1987
Manage your Time	(L)	Garratt, Sally	Fontana, 1985
Rethinking the Future	(M)	Edited by Gibson, Rowan	Nicholas Brealey, 1997
The Goal – A Process of Ongoing Improvement	(H)	Goldratt, Eliyahu & Cox, Jeff	Gower, 1993
The Hallmarks for Successful Business, 2nd edition	(L)	Hall, David	Management Books 2000, 2002
The Empty Raincoat – Making Sense of the Future	(M)	Hardy, Charles	Hutchinson, 1994
Superteams – A Blueprint for Organisational Success	(L)	Hastings, Colin, Bixby, Peter & Chaudistry-Lawton, Rani	Fontana, 1986
Requisite Organization – a total system for effective managerial organization and managerial leadership for the 21st century	(H)	Jaques, Elliott	Carson Hall, 1998
Exploring Corporate Strategy	(H)	Johnson, Gerry& Scholes, Kevan	Prentice Hall, 1988
Managerial Breakthrough	(H)	Juran, J M	McGraw Hill, 1964
The Balanced Scorecard	(H)	Kaplan, Robert S & Norton, David P	HBS Press, 1996

Title	L/M/H	Author	Publisher/Year
Managing Negotiations, 2nd Edition	(M)	Kennedy, Gavin, Benson, John & McMillan, John	Business Books, 1985
The New Rational Manager	(H)	Kepner, Charles H & Tregoe, Benjamin B	John Martin, 1981
Live to Win – achieving success in Life and Business	(L)	Kiam, Victor	Harper & Row, 1989
The Roots of Excellence	(L)	Lessem, Ronnie	Fontana, 1985
The Change Masters – Corporate Entrepreneurs at Work	(H)	Moss-Kanter, Rosabeth	Counterpoint Unwins, 1985
New Office Technology – Human and Organizational Aspects	(H)	Edited by Otway, Harry J & Peltu, Malcolm	Francis Pinter, 1983
The Shorter MBA – a practical approach to Business Skills	(M)	Edited by Pearson, Barrier & Thomas, Neil	Thorsons, 1991
Managing Yourself	(L)	Pedler, Mike & Boydell, Tom	Fontana, 1985
A Managers Guide to self development, 3rd Edition	(L)	Pedler, Mike, Burgoyne, John & Boydell, Tom	McGraw Hill, 1994
Action Learning for Managers	(L)	Pedler, Mike	Lemos & Crane, 1996
The Learning Company – a strategy for sustainable development, 2nd Edition	(L)	Pedler, Mike, Burgoyne, John & Boydell, Tom	McGraw Hill, 1997
A Concise Guide to the Learning Organisation – Managing Change and learning is the No 1 task – wherever you work	(M)	Pedler, Mike & Aspinall, Kath	Lemos & Crane, 1998
A Passion for Excellence – The Leadership Difference	(M)	Peters, Tom	Fontana, 1986
Thriving on Chaos – a handbook for management revolution	(M)	Peters, Tom	MacMillan, 1988
Managing Change and Making it Stick	(L)	Plant, Roger	Fontana, 1987

Title	L/M/H	Author	Publisher/Year
Organisational Design – The Work-Levels Approach	(H)	Rowbottom, Ralph & Billis, David	Gower, 1987
Organizational Culture and Leadership	(H)	Schein, Edgar H	Jossey Bass, 1986
Process Consultation – Lessons for Managers and Consultants (Vol II)	(H)	Schein, Edgar H	Addison Wesley, 1987
The Fifth Discipline Fieldbook – strategies and tools for building a learning organisation	(H)	Senge, Peter	Nicholas Brealey, 1994
The Dance of Change – The Challenge of Sustaining momentum in Learning Organisations	(H)	Senge, Peter	Nicholas Brealey, 1999
The 10-Day MBA – a step by step guide to mastering the skills taught in top business schools	(M)	Silbiger, Steven	Piatkus, 1999
Team Spirit	(L)	Syer, John	Simon & Schuster, 1989
54 Approaches to Brickwall Management – Managing Change at Work	(L)	Wash, Michael	Management Books 2000, 2006
Organisational Development for the NHS	(M)	Wash, Michael	www.mwauk.com
Organizational Diagnosis: A workbook of Theory and Practice	(M)	Weisbord, Marvin R	Addison Wesley, 1987
Winning	(M)	Welch, Jack	Harper Collins, 2005
Leadership and the New Science – Discovering order in a chaotic world	(H)	Wheatley, Margaret J	Berrett Koehler Pub. Ltd 2006
The Ascendant Organisation	(H)	Wickens, Peter D	Macmillan, 1995

Useful Websites

www.bestforbusiness.com	Wide portfolio of advice about matters concerning the management of a business.
www.businessballs.com	Comprehensive access to a wide range of business techniques, resources and suppliers.
www.changingminds.org	Extensive information on all aspects of influencing skills, techniques and approaches.
www.denisonconsulting.com	A company offering surveys and tools about culture and leadership.
www.developingmanagers-uk.co.uk	Offers courses for first line managers.
www.indigobusiness.co.uk	European Distributor for Dr Edward De Bono's work. Offers workshops focusing creative and lateral thinking, plus many other management skills and techniques.
www.managementhelp.org	Offering a 'free' management library on all matters of management and business skills.
www.managementtoday.co.uk	Current thinking on the management issues of the day.
www.mindtools.com	One of the most extensive and practically helpful sites for the developing manager.
www.quality.co.uk	For all aspects of quality management, including Benchmarking.
www.smartdraw.com	From flowcharts to Gantt charts; business graphics software.
www.thequalityportal.com	All topics related to 'quality management'.
www.tutor2u.net	Business and organisation development resources including blogs, quizzes and forums.

Bibliography

Adair, J., *Action Centred Leadership*, Gower, 1982

Adair, J., *Effective Teambuilding*, Pan Books, 1987

Argyris, C., *Overcoming Organizational Defences*, Prentice – Hall, 1990

Bennis, W., *Leaders – The Strategies for Taking Charge*, Harper & Row, 1985

Bion, W. R., *Experiences in Groups*, Tavistock, 1961

Broom, M. F., *The Infinite Organization: Celebrating the Positive Use of Power in Organizations*, Davies-Black Publishing, 2002

Checkland, P., *Systems Thinking, Systems Practice*, John Wiley & Sons, 1981

Connor, M., & Pokora, J., *Coaching and Mentoring at Work – Developing Effective Practice*, McGraw Hill in association with Open University Press, 2007

De Bono, E., *Six Thinking Hats*, Penguin, 1985

Egan, G., *Adding Value: A Systematic Guide to Business-Driven Management and Leadership*, Jossey Bass, 1993

Egan, G., *The Skilled Helper – a problem management approach to helping*, Brooks Cole, 6th edition, 1998

Hersey, P. & Blanchard, K., *Management of Organisation Behaviour*, Prentice Hall, 1982

Ingham, H. & Luft, J., 'The Johari window, a graphic model of interpersonal awareness', *Proceedings of the western training laboratory in group development*, Los Angeles: UCLA, 1955

Ishikawa, K., Lu. D. J. trans., *What is Total Quality Control?*, Prentice Hall Inc, Englewood Cliffs, NJ, 1985

Juran, J. M., *Managerial Breakthrough*, McGraw Hill, 1964

Lewin, K., *Field Theory in Social Science*, Harper and Row, NY, 1951

Likert, R. A., *Technique for the Measurement of Attitudes*, Archives of Psychology 140, 55. 1932

Mcgregor, D., *The Human Side of Enterprise*, McGraw Hill 1960

Pareto, Vilfredo, 1848–1923 (In Juran 1964)

Pedler, M., & Burgoyne J., & Boydell T., *The Learning Company – a strategy for sustainable development, 2nd Edition,* McGraw Hill, 1997

Rasiel, E. & Friga, P., *The McKinsey Mind: Understanding and Implementing the Problem-Solving Tools and Management Techniques of the World's Top Strategic Consulting Firm,* McGraw Hill, 2001

Revans, R., *Abc Of Action Learning*, Lemos & Crane (UK), 1998

Wash, M., *54 Approaches to Brickwall Management – Managing Change at Work*, Management Books 2000, 2006

Whitmore, J., *Coaching for Performance: GROWing People, Performance and Purpose*, 3rd Edition, Nicholas Brealey, 2002

Index of Tools and Techniques

About the Author

I have been in the business of helping individuals and organisations realise their full potential for over 20 years.

My early career as a psychiatric nurse gave me great fascination and insight into the extremes of human behaviour. From nursing I progressed to teaching psychiatry, psychology and counselling within the UK Health Service. During this period, I also qualified as a psychotherapist, and co-authored a best selling text book, *Psychiatric Nursing Skills,* a client-centred approach, first published by Chapman Hall in 1986 (the second edition was published in 2000 by Nelson Thornes).

I became restless within my teaching position and began questioning whether my skills and experience could be applied elsewhere, as at the time, in the early 80's, the Health Service seemed to be a gigantic and less than dynamic monolith, and I was ready to spread my wings.

I wrote a paper with the proposition that senior executives in large organisations were probably deluded at best, and at worst, psychotic – given that very few could possibly understand the impact they had on others. This paper gave me several interviews, one of which led to a job offer which transformed my working life. I became a member of the internal consulting team in British Telecom.

Here I learnt my business acumen, dovetailing my caring, teaching and counselling skills to an organisation agenda desperate for change. During this period, I also completed my Masters Degree in Business and Economics, researching the effectiveness of leadership behaviour in service industry.

After 5 years on a very steep learning curve, it became apparent that I was best suited as a free agent – I left and set up my own business in 1989.

Apart from 2 years employed as an Organisation Development Director for a large teaching hospital, my work has primarily been consulting to organisations whose quest included how to recover from crisis, how to build a team, how to transform an organisation and how to change a culture.

I have had the privilege of working with many great organisations and enjoyed the freedom and vulnerability of the travelling consultant. I can't envisage a time when I will tire from working with those people who have a thirst and passion to change, learn, improve and realise their ambition for a better way of working and a healthier, balanced lifestyle.

Clients' Comments

"Mike Wash is a highly responsive consultant with a track record of working within complex environments. He has helped us introduce our 'Excellence through Learning' programme across the whole organisation aimed at delivering culture change and sustainable performance improvement. The Trust won the 2006 National HRM awards for developing a Learning Organisation approach toward organisational change."

Tony Bell, Chief Executive, Royal Liverpool Children's NHS Trust - Alder Hey

"The feedback from both the consultancy work Mike performed and the leadership workshops he ran was quite extraordinary. Mike's interventions have assisted ABS to improve its productivity as well as increasing both turnover and profitability."

Chris Bunker, HR Director, ABS Wastewater Technology Limited

"The best consultants don't just give you what they have got; they give you what you need. In all the year's I have known Mike I have found him incredibly resourceful in finding an approach that fitted the question we had as a business."

Graham Higgins, Head of Learning and Development, Cathay Pacific Airways

Other Publications by Michael Wash

54 Approaches to Brickwall Management
Managing Change at Work

(164 pages • £14.99)

Have you ever wondered why it is so hard to get people to buy in to what seems to be a sensible, or even brilliant, new idea or way of doing things?

Have you ever felt a little uneasy or unsettled when asked to do something new or change something you have been doing for years?

Have you ever wondered why people react in many sometimes strange, and obstructive, ways to events at work – that should be seen as work?

Have you ever had self doubt about presenting something that maybe new or challenging to your audience?

In this book, I have tried to illustrate the varied approaches (sometime not effective) that people adopt to get others to do things they may initially resist. These approaches also challenge the reader to look at themselves and their own willingness to be open to change.

The situations cover many work related (some would say life related) incidents, such as redundancy, stress, imposed new systems, change of job, bullying, promotion and many more.

In addition to these are exercises to give you feedback on your effectiveness in managing your personal development, time management, meeting effectiveness and how you work as a team. A questionnaire on leadership will help you gain insight into your own style of influencing others.

Every manager and supervisor should read this book and if your organisation has courage, and wants to create a healthy, thriving work environment, then pass the book on to your staff and ask them to choose an approach which they would like to discuss!!

Good luck in dismantling your brickwalls!

Published by Management Books 2000 in 2006.

For further details visit www.mb2000.com

Coming soon

54 Approaches to Organisational Healing
54 Simple Truths with Brutal Advice

For further information visit www.mwauk.com